Collins New Primary Maths

Pupil Book 5B

Series Editor: Peter Clarke

Authors: Jeanette Mumford, Sandra Roberts, Andrew Edmondson

Contents

Unit A2

		Page number
Lesson 1	All in order	4-5
Lesson 2	Flying kites	6-7
Lesson 3	Flying balloons	8-9
Lesson 4	Problems, problems	10-11
Lesson 5	And more problems!	12-13
Lesson 6	Doubles and halves	14-15
Lesson 7	Using division facts	16-17
Lesson 8	10, 100 and 1000	18-19
Lesson 9	Multiplying by 12, 19 and 21	20-21
Lesson 10	Calculator challenge	22-23

Unit B2

Lesson 1	Adding and subtracting in your head	24-25
Lesson 2	Growing calculations	26-27
Lesson 3	Finding out about odd and even numbers	28-29
Lesson 4	At the cinema	30-31
Lesson 5	In your head	32-33
Lesson 6	Order of operations	34-35
Lesson 7	Doubling and halving whole numbers	36-37
Lesson 8	Decimal doubles and halves	38-39
Lesson 9	Sorting numbers by divisibility	40-41
Lesson 10	Counting in steps of 25	42-43
Lesson 11	All sorts of triangles	44-45
Lesson 12	Symmetry in triangles	46-47
Lesson 13	Reflective symmetry in regular polygons	48-49
Lesson 14	Perpendicular and parallel lines	50-51
Lesson 15	Reflecting 2-D shapes	52-53

Unit C2

Lesson 1	Using standard weights	54-55
Lesson 2	Using scales	56-57
Lesson 3	Rounding weights	58-59
Lesson 4	Personal databases	60-61
Lesson 5	Football bar line charts	62-63
Lesson 6	Line graphs	64-65
Lesson 7	Multiplication line graphs	66-67

		Page number
Lesson 8	Temperature line graphs	68-69
Lesson 9	Chance	70-71
Lesson 10	Take a chance	72-73

Unit D2

Lesson 1	Solve the problems	74-75
Lesson 2	Calculate decimals and fractions	76-77
Lesson 3	Multiplying and dividing by 10, 100 and 1000	78-79
Lesson 4	Reviewing multiplication	80-81
Lesson 5	Key it in	82-83
Lesson 6	Plotting and constructing	84-85
Lesson 7	Measuring angles	86-87
Lesson 8	Calculating areas	88-89
Lesson 9	Shopping in kilograms	90-91
Lesson 10	Cooking up problems	92-93

Unit E2

Lesson 1	Decimal sums and differences	94-95
Lesson 2	Find the equivalent	96-97
Lesson 3	Using diagrams	98-99
Lesson 4	Find my partner	100-101
Lesson 5	Fractions, decimals and percentages	102-103
Lesson 6	Percentage problems	104-105
Lesson 7	In proportion	106-107
Lesson 8	Use the proportion	108-109
Lesson 9	Divide and share	110-111
Lesson 10	Calculating costs	112-113
Lesson 11	Doubling multiplication facts	114-115
Lesson 12	Doubling and halving whole numbers and decimals	116-117
Lesson 13	Exchange rates	118-119
Lesson 14	Using a calculator	120-121
Lesson 15	Number puzzles	122-123
	Maths Facts	124-127

All in order

Explain what each digit represents in whole numbers and decimals with up to two decimal places

1 Copy and complete the number lines. The first one is done for you.

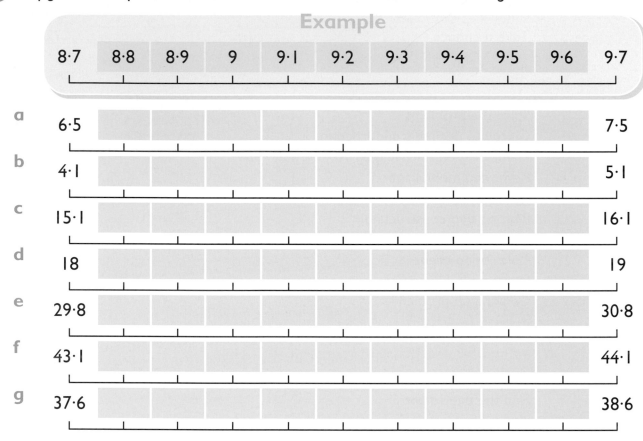

Example

| 8·7 | 8·8 | 8·9 | 9 | 9·1 | 9·2 | 9·3 | 9·4 | 9·5 | 9·6 | 9·7 |

a 6·5 ... 7·5

b 4·1 ... 5·1

c 15·1 ... 16·1

d 18 ... 19

e 29·8 ... 30·8

f 43·1 ... 44·1

g 37·6 ... 38·6

2 Order these groups of decimals from smallest to largest.

a	b	c	d	e
6·3	6·7	13·8	81·7	25·6
7·3	9·1	13·1	18·1	24·7
3·6	9·5	14	81·2	25·8
5·6	5·1	14·3	18·5	23·9
7·6	5·9	13·6	18·7	25·2

3 Look at the red digits in questions **2** **d** and **e**. Write down what they represent.

1 Copy and complete the number lines. The first one is done for you.

Example

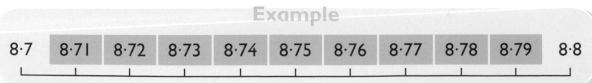

| 8·7 | 8·71 | 8·72 | 8·73 | 8·74 | 8·75 | 8·76 | 8·77 | 8·78 | 8·79 | 8·8 |

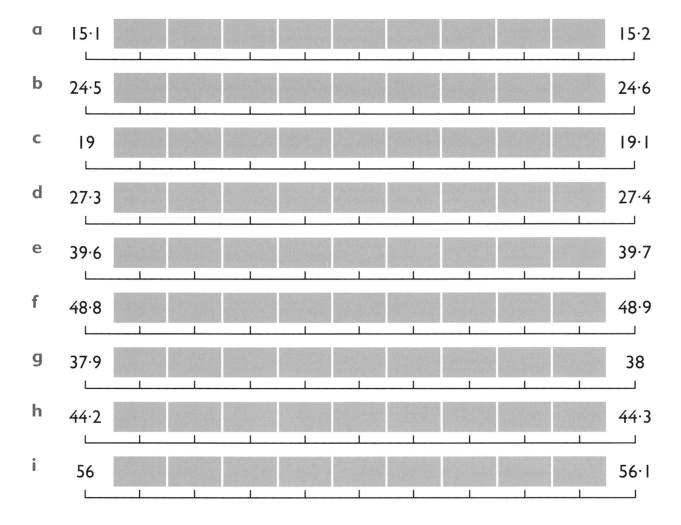

a 15·1 — 15·2

b 24·5 — 24·6

c 19 — 19·1

d 27·3 — 27·4

e 39·6 — 39·7

f 48·8 — 48·9

g 37·9 — 38

h 44·2 — 44·3

i 56 — 56·1

2 Order these groups of decimals from smallest to largest.

a	b	c	d	e
6·85	19·04	35·09	46·13	67·92
6·58	19·08	35·99	64·33	68·98
6·88	20·01	35·19	46·31	60·90
6·55	19·28	35·29	44·30	86·94
6·80	20·48	35·89	46·03	76·93
6·50	20·14	35·90	64·23	80·09

3 Look at the red digits in question **2** d and e. Write down what they represent.

 Write the decimals in question **2** of the activity as fractions.

Example

$6·85 = 6\frac{85}{100}$

Flying kites

- **Use knowledge of place value and subtraction of two-digit numbers to derive differences**
- **Use efficient written methods to subtract whole numbers**

Find the difference between each pair of numbers.
First subtract the tens and then the units. Record
your method as calculations.

Example

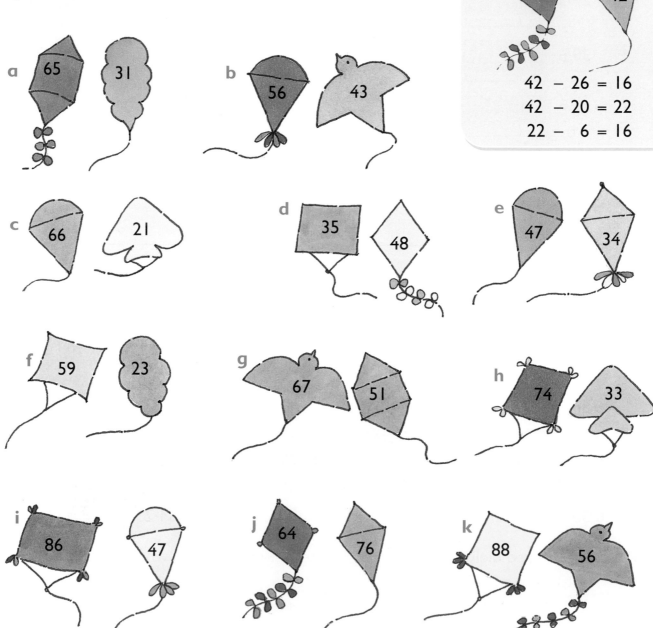

42 − 26 = 16
42 − 20 = 22
22 − 6 = 16

a 65 31

b 56 43

c 66 21

d 35 48

e 47 34

f 59 23

g 67 51

h 74 33

i 86 47

j 64 76

k 88 56

1 Write fifteen subtraction calculations using these numbers. Choose the best method to work them out. Show all your workings.

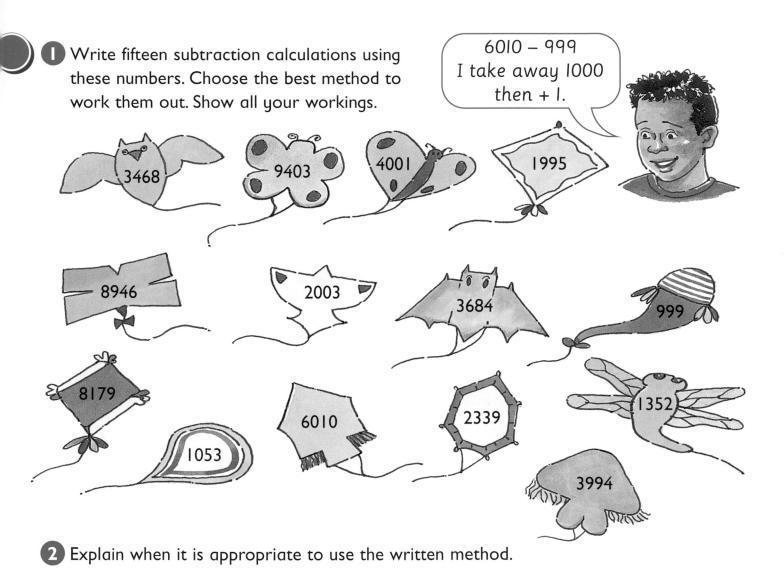

6010 – 999
I take away 1000
then + 1.

3468
9403
4001
1995
8946
2003
3684
999
8179
6010
1053
2339
1352
3994

2 Explain when it is appropriate to use the written method.

I always use the written method for any subtraction calculation that I do.

How would you persuade him that this is not always the most efficient method?

Flying balloons

- **Use knowledge of place value and addition of two-digit numbers to derive sums**
- **Use efficient written methods to add whole numbers**

Find the sum of each pair of numbers. First add the tens and then the units. Record your methods as calculations.

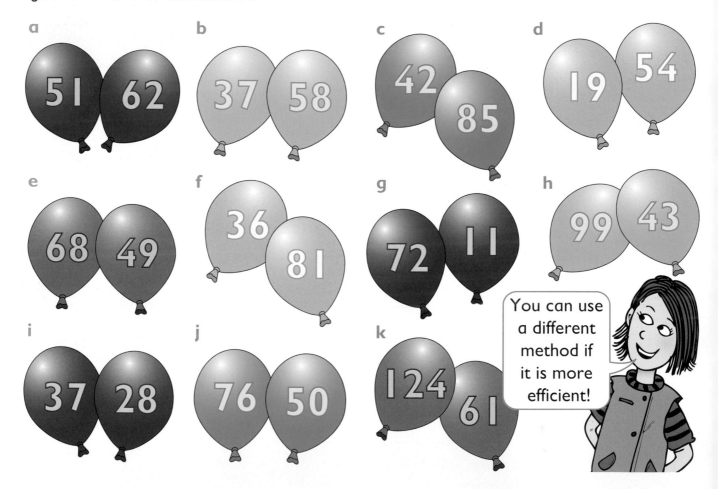

a   51   62

b   37   58

c   42   85

d   19   54

e   68   49

f   36   81

g   72   11

h   99   43

You can use a different method if it is more efficient!

i   37   28

j   76   50

k   124   61

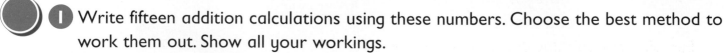

1 Write fifteen addition calculations using these numbers. Choose the best method to work them out. Show all your workings.

104   542   1642

2 Explain how you decided which method to use.

The total is 500. Can you find ten different ways to make that total adding three different three-digit numbers? Multiples of ten or a hundred are not allowed!

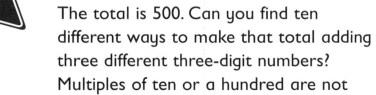

Problems, problems

Work out the answers to these word problems. Write the calculations you need to work out each problem.

a Katie and her sister are having a party. Katie wants to invite 36 friends and her sister wants to invite 47 friends. How many invitations do they need altogether?

b The school kitchen cooked 86 pizzas. 39 got eaten, how many were left?

c There are 204 people on the train. 98 get off at the first station. How many passengers are left on the train?

d I think of a number. I add 35 and the answer is 51. What number was I thinking of?

e 145 people have visited the museum so far today. There is a group of 47 children coming this afternoon. What will the total number of visitors be?

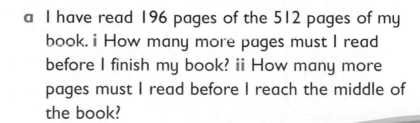

Work out the answers to these word problems. Write the calculations you need to work out each problem.

a I have read 196 pages of the 512 pages of my book. i How many more pages must I read before I finish my book? ii How many more pages must I read before I reach the middle of the book?

b I think of a number. I add 74 and then 56. The answer is 197. **i** What was my number? **ii** What do I need to add to 197 to get 702?

c 7006 people visited the museum last year. So far, 4991 people have visited this year. The museum has predicted that there will be 3020 more visitors this year. What will be the difference between the two years' totals?

d A lorry can hold 205 boxes. The driver has put in 42 boxes at one pick-up and 67 at another. **i** How many more boxes does he have space for? **ii** If there were two full lorries how many boxes would they have?

e The total length of the playground is 245 metres. The football area is 75 metres long and the grassy area is 96 metres long. What is the length of the rest of the playground?

Make up some word problems about your class and your school. Try to make them two-step problems. Use these calculations.

a $69 - 23 - ? = 12$

b $48 + 96 + ? = 203$

c $712 - 496 - ? = 109$

d $176 + ? + 204 = 478$

And more problems!

Work out the answers to these word problems using a written method.

a I buy two tickets for the match. They cost £12.67 each. How much did I spend?

b I have £17.45 and I spend £8.71 on a present for my mum. How much will I have left?

c I earn £6.78 a week for my Saturday job. How much will I have after three weeks?

d I have saved £12.94 but my sister has saved £5.35 more than me. How much does she have?

e If I spent £4.99 on Monday and £3.42 on Tuesday how much have I spent altogether?

1 Work out the answers to these word problems using a written method.

a I spent £14.26 on some books and £13.87 on a bag. I had £1.13 left. How much money did I have to start with?

You need:
● calculator

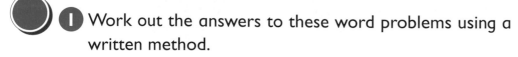
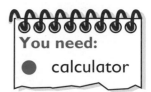

b In the first half hour of opening, the sweet shop took £29.86 from customers. £12.73 is given back in change altogether. How much is left in the till?

c I start the day out with £17.39 in my purse. I spend £4.68 on my lunch and I go to the cinema. When I get home I have £8.37 left. How much did the cinema cost?

2 Work out the answers to these word problems using a calculator.

a I want to buy five T-shirts since they are on special offer. They are £3.99 each. What change will I get from a £20 note?

b The class has collected £40 towards their outing. The children's tickets will cost £33.47 altogether. Two teachers are going and their tickets cost £1.35 each. How much money will be left?

c I want a coat which is priced at £59.98 and some shoes priced £38.56. The shop reduces everything by half. How much will the two items cost now?

Which amounts up to £1 cannot be paid exactly with fewer than 6 coins?

Doubles and halves

 1 Copy and complete.

a   4·3,   4·4,   4·5,   4·6,   ☐ ,   ☐ ,   ☐ ,   ☐ ,   ☐ ,   ☐ .

b   0·2,   0·4,   0·6,   0·8,   ☐ ,   ☐ ,   ☐ ,   ☐ ,   ☐ ,   ☐ .

c   5,   4·7,   4·4,   4·1,   ☐ ,   ☐ ,   ☐ ,   ☐ ,   ☐ ,   ☐ .

d   7·2,   7·5,   7·8,   8·1,   ☐ ,   ☐ ,   ☐ ,   ☐ ,   ☐ ,   ☐ .

e   9,   8·6,   8·2,   7·8,   ☐ ,   ☐ ,   ☐ ,   ☐ ,   ☐ ,   ☐ .

2 Double each decimal.

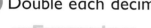

Example

$2·4 × 2 = 4·8$

8·3

4·2   7·1

5·4   8·4

2·4

4·5   6·1

9·2

0·3

3 Halve each decimal.

Example

$\frac{1}{2} × 0·46 = 0·23$

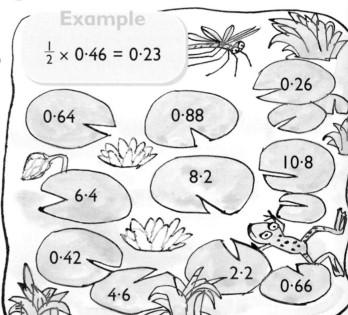

0·26

0·64   0·88

10·8

8·2

6·4

0·42

2·2   0·66

4·6

5·6   7·2   4·7   2·8

8·9   6·4

3·1   9·4   1·5   6·3

0·88

0·47   0·26

0·63

0·12   0·35

0·34   0·91   0·79   0·57

● Find all the decimals with one place. Double them.

Example

5·6 × 2
5·0 × 2 = 10
0·6 × 2 = 1·2
10 + 1·2 = 11·2

2 Find all the decimals with one place. Halve them.

Example

5·6 ÷ 2
5·0 ÷ 2 = 2·5
0·6 ÷ 2 = 0·3
2·5 + 0·3 = 2·8

3 Find all the decimals with two places. Double them.

Example

0·47 × 2
0·4 × 2 = 0·8
0·07 × 2 = 0·14
0·8 + 0·14 = 0·94

● Copy and complete the diagrams to show that halving is the inverse of doubling.

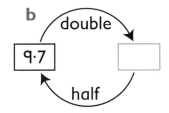

a ×2   6·3 □   ÷2

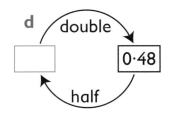

b double   9·7 □   half

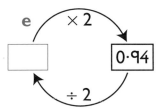

c ×2   □ 0·72   ÷2

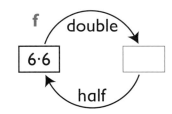

d double   □ 0·48   half

e ×2   □ 0·94   ÷2

f double   6·6 □   half

Play the doubles game!

A game for 2 players.

● Place the number cards face down in a pile.
● Turn over the top card. Both players write the number down.
● Start the minute timer. Double the number and keep doubling your answer until the minute is up.
● Compare your answers. The player with the most correct numbers scores 1 point.
● The first player to reach 10 points is the winner.

You need:

● about 20 tenths number cards from 1·1 to 9·9
● a 1-minute timer
● paper and pencil

Using division facts

• **Use multiplication and division facts to divide pairs of multiples of 10 and 100**

 ① Copy and complete.

a 28 ÷ 4 = ○   i 81 ÷ 9 = ○

b 48 ÷ 6 = ○   j 56 ÷ 8 = ○

c 27 ÷ 3 = ○   k 18 ÷ 6 = ○

d 18 ÷ 2 = ○   l 24 ÷ 3 = ○

e 54 ÷ 6 = ○   m 45 ÷ 9 = ○

f 30 ÷ 3 = ○   n 60 ÷ 6 = ○

g 32 ÷ 4 = ○   o 72 ÷ 9 = ○

h 8 ÷ 2 = ○   p 40 ÷ 10 = ○

② Write all the pairs of factors for each of the following numbers.

a 56   b 28   c 48   d 66   e 30   f 82

 ① Copy and complete each set of calculations.

a
24 ÷ 4
2400 ÷ 4
240 ÷ 40

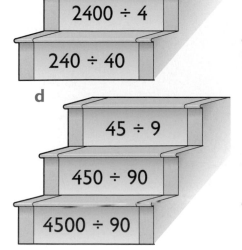

b
54 ÷ 6
5400 ÷ 60
54000 ÷ 600

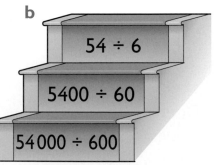

c
18 ÷ 3
1800 ÷ 300
18000 ÷ 30

d
45 ÷ 9
450 ÷ 90
4500 ÷ 90

e
21 ÷ 7
21000 ÷ 7000
2100 ÷ 70

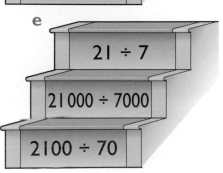

f
64 ÷ 8
64000 ÷ 800
6400 ÷ 8

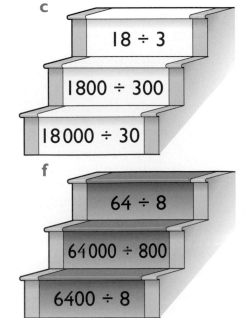

2 Use your knowledge of the division facts to help you work out the answers to these calculations.

a 24 000 ÷ 40 = ☐   i 60 000 ÷ 300 = ☐

b 18 000 ÷ 300 = ☐   j 3600 ÷ 6 = ☐

c 3500 ÷ 5 = ☐   k 7200 ÷ 900 = ☐

d 1800 ÷ 20 = ☐   l 3500 ÷ 70 = ☐

e 4200 ÷ 60 = ☐   m 1600 ÷ 40 = ☐

f 5000 ÷ 500 = ☐   n 30 000 ÷ 300 = ☐

g 640 ÷ 80 = ☐   o 2400 ÷ 800 = ☐

h 12 000 ÷ 20 = ☐   p 600 ÷ 10 = ☐

 **1** Copy and complete.

a ☐ ÷ 30 = 600   f 35 000 ÷ ☐ = 700

b ☐ ÷ 800 = 40   g 540 ÷ ☐ = 9

c 3000 ÷ ☐ = 500   h ☐ ÷ 900 = 20

d 4900 ÷ ☐ = 7   i ☐ ÷ 400 = 40

e ☐ ÷ 3 = 60   j 48 000 ÷ ☐ = 600

2 Write 10 other multiplication or division facts that are related to 56 ÷ 7 = 8.

I know that 56 ÷ 7 = 8. I used this to work out that 560 ÷ 7 = 80.

10, 100 and 1000

- Multiply and divide by 10, 100 and 1000 and understand the effect

 1 Multiply each of these by 10.

652

54

2527

574

2 Multiply each of these by 100.

75

3

1247

862

3 Divide each of these by 10.

5310

420

700

862

4 Divide each of these by 100.

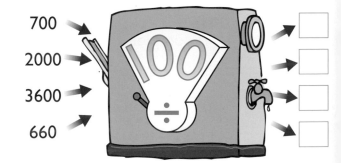

700

2000

3600

660

 1 Multiply and divide each of these numbers by 10.

a 30	e 600	i 5300
b 65	f 820	j 3452
c 4	g 433	k 1620
d 950	h 3000	l 32 440

Example

560 × 10 = 5600

560 ÷ 10 = 56

2 Multiply and divide each of these numbers by 100.

a 42	e 700	i 6543
b 7	f 367	j 84 000
c 60	g 8420	k 71 230
d 470	h 3500	l 95 378

65 × 10 = ?
820 ÷ 10 = ?

7 × 100
? ?
7 ÷ 100

● Multiply and divide each of these numbers by 1000.

a 650   c 300   e 6400

b 920   d 8000   f 9840

4 Multiply and divide each of these decimals by 10.

a 5·8   e 12·3   i 685·2

b 6·4   f 85·7   j 415·4

c 4·9   g 34·6   k 325·6

d 3·7   h 91·2   l 956·8

Example

$6·3 \times 10 = 63$

$6·3 \div 10 = 0·63$

1 How many times larger is 3400 than 34?

2 How many £10 notes are in £340? How many £10 notes in £3400?

3 Packets of biscuits that cost 51p each are put in boxes of 100. How much does each box cost? How much do 10 boxes cost?

4 How many times smaller is 28 than 28 000?

5 Each bag of sweets contains 14 sweets.

I have 140 sweets, so how many bags did I buy? What if I had 1400 sweets?

Multiplying by 12, 19 and 21

● **Extend mental methods for whole number calculations**

a 12 × 9
b 12 × 15
c 12 × 6
d 12 × 8
e 12 × 13

f 12 × 16
g 12 × 22
h 12 × 25
i 12 × 31
j 12 × 28

k 12 × 40
l 12 × 50
m 12 × 35
n 12 × 28
o 12 × 36

Remember

A quick way to multiply by 12 is:

$$12 × 7 = (10 × 7) + (2 × 7)$$
$$= 70 + 14$$
$$= 84$$

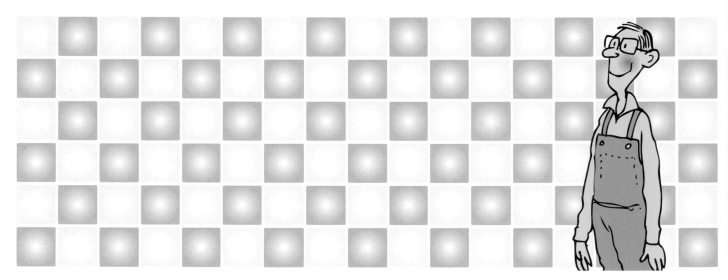

 1 Calculate the answers to these. Show your working.

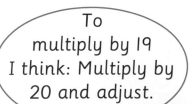
To multiply by 19 I think: Multiply by 20 and adjust.

a 8 × 19
b 6 × 19
c 17 × 19
d 13 × 19
e 15 × 19

f 23 × 19
g 35 × 19
h 45 × 19
i 48 × 19
j 67 × 19

Example

$$12 × 19 = (12 × 20) - 12$$
$$= 240 - 12$$
$$= 228$$

To multiply by 21 I think: Multiply by 20 and adjust.

2 Calculate the answers to these. Show your working.

a 9 × 21   f 36 × 21
b 14 × 21   g 39 × 21
c 18 × 21   h 43 × 21
d 25 × 21   i 52 × 21
e 27 × 21   j 68 × 21

Example

13 × 21 = (13 × 20) + 13
        = 260 + 13
        = 273

Mr and Mrs Oldham bought tiles for their kitchen floor.

Tile prices

Y £19   W £21

G £20   B £9

Prepare an invoice showing:
- the total cost for each colour tile
- the total cost for tiling the floor

INVOICE

TILES
YELLOW
WHITE
GREEN
BLUE

TOTAL

Calculator challenge

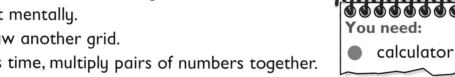

Develop calculator skills and use a calculator effectively

 1 Draw a 4 x 4 grid.

   a Add pairs of the blue numbers together. Try mentally first. Use your calculator if you need to.

   b Write your answers in the grid.

   c Circle the answer if you calculated it mentally.

2 Draw another grid.
This time, multiply pairs of numbers together.

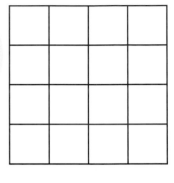

9   15   60   75   41   6   200

You need:
● calculator

 1 A game for 2 players.

● Take turns to add two of the purple numbers together. Try mentally first, then use your calculator. You are aiming to get one of the grid numbers.

● Place one of your counters on the number in the grid if you calculate it. The first player with three numbers in a row, column or diagonal wins.

● Use your calculator to add up the grid numbers you have placed a counter on. Who has got the larger total?

You need:
● calculator
● 24 small counters: 12 in one colour and 12 in another colour

50   126   100   74

305

65	690	87	373	290
93	259	194	500	755
142	69	340	145	172
26	114	118	366	107
124	314	75	176	200

240

450

7

19

46   33   68

2 Play the game using this grid.
Subtract these numbers.

8   16   92
300   135
20   101
            47

84	119	81	253
208	45	199	43
31	88	93	4
9	27	115	76

3 Multiply these numbers.

19   100   36
5   31   7
11   10

3100	209	217	55
1116	77	190	700
180	396	1000	133
35	155	589	110

1 A game for 2 players.

Copy the number grid.

146
51   92
29
40   17
    235

95	197	143	75
381	206	89	80
46	275	106	121
11	63	286	195

You need:

● calculator
● coloured pencil

2 Go back and take turns to calculate the missing grid numbers.
Circle each one with your colour.

3 Use your calculator to add up the grid numbers you have circled. Who got the largest total?

● Take turns to add or subtract two of the red numbers. Try mentally first. Then use your calculator. You are aiming to get one of the grid numbers.
● Circle a grid number you calculate.
● The first person to circle three numbers in a row, column or diagonal wins.

Adding and subtracting in your head

 Work out the calculations. Use your number facts to help you.

a 6 + 4
  60 + 40
  600 + 400

b 5 + 3
  50 + 30
  500 + 300

c 6 + 7
  60 + 70
  600 + 700

d 9 + 3
  90 + 30
  900 + 300

e 12 + 4
  120 + 40

f 13 + 5
  130 + 50

g 9 − 4
  90 − 40
  900 − 400

h 8 − 3
  80 − 30
  800 − 300

i 7 − 5
  70 − 50
  700 − 500

j 18 − 6
  180 − 60

k 17 − 5
  170 − 50

l 15 − 4
  150 − 40

 Work out the first calculation and use it to help you work out the other two.

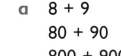

a 8 + 9
  80 + 90
  800 + 900

b 13 − 7
  130 − 70
  1300 − 700

c 14 + 5
  140 + 50
  1400 + 500

d 19 − 4
  190 − 40
  1900 − 400

e 6 + 7 + 4
  60 + 70 + 40
  600 + 700 + 400

f 8 + 9 + 7
  80 + 90 + 70
  800 + 900 + 700

g 5 + 3 + 7
  50 + 30 + 70
  500 + 300 + 700

h 26 − 18
  260 − 180
  2600 − 1800

i 3 + 9 + 6
  30 + 90 + 60
  300 + 900 + 600

2 Work out the first calculation and use it to help you work out the other two.

a   2 + 5 + 8 + 3
   20 + 50 + 80 + 30
   200 + 500 + 800 + 300

b   6 + 7 + 2 + 4
   60 + 70 + 20 + 40
   600 + 700 + 200 + 400

c   80 + 10 + 90 + 50
   8 + 1 + 9 + 5
   800 + 100 + 900 + 500

d   600 + 400 + 700 + 300
   60 + 40 + 70 + 30
   6 + 4 + 7 + 3

e   800 + 100 + 300 + 500
   8 + 1 + 3 + 5
   80 + 10 + 30 + 50

f   9 + 4 + 7 + 5 + 6
   900 + 400 + 700 + 500 + 600
   90 + 40 + 70 + 50 + 60

g   30 + 40 + 80 + 60 + 90
   3 + 4 + 8 + 6 + 9
   300 + 400 + 800 + 600 + 900

h   700 + 800 + 400 + 500 + 200
   70 + 80 + 40 + 50 + 20
   7 + 8 + 4 + 5 + 2

3 Now choose one calculation from each section and explain how you worked it out. You can use numbers or words.

Write 1500 in the middle of your page. Think of as many addition or subtraction calculations where the answer is 1500. Make them as different as possible.

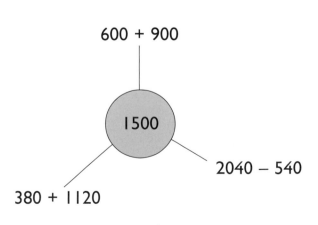

600 + 900

1500

2040 − 540

380 + 1120

Growing calculations

 Work out the answer to the calculation in the middle, then think of other calculations that go with it.

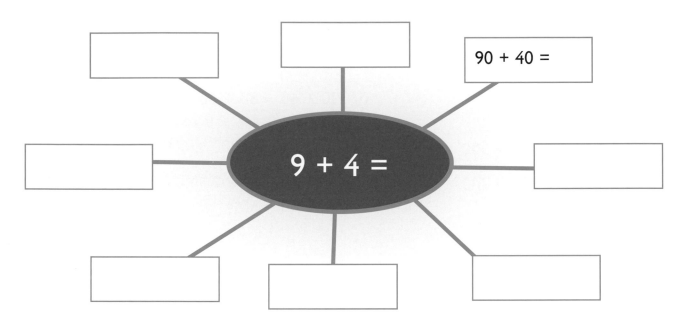

90 + 40 =

9 + 4 =

 Work out the answer to the calculation in the middle, then think of other calculations that go with it.

I

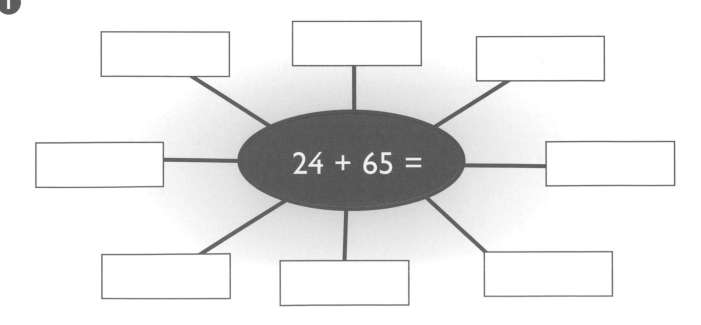

24 + 65 =

2

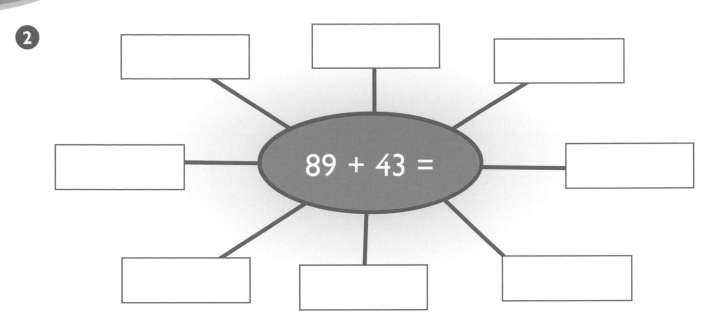

89 + 43 =

3 Look at your answers for question **2**. Explain why all these calculations go together.

 Design a diagram for your classroom to illustrate the relationship of the place value of the calculations you have worked on today.

Finding out about odd and even numbers

 1 Copy and complete each table by finding numbers that fit.

a

Even

+	4	6	10
6	10		
8			
2			

(Even)

b

Odd

+	3	7	
5			

(Odd)

c

Odd

+			

(Even)

2 Match each statement below with the correct table.

Odd + odd = even

Even + even = even

Odd + even = odd

 Use the numbers shown to complete these statements. Provide examples to prove your statements.

HINT

Try five examples before making a general statement.

a The sum of three even numbers is ☐.

 26 14

64

73 27

e The difference between one odd number and one even number is ☐

d The difference between 2 even numbers is ☐.

b The difference between two odd numbers is ☐.

c The sum of any odd number and any even number is ☐.

g The sum of 4 odd numbers is ☐.

42

95

51

69

58

89

13

47

100

35

f The sum of three odd numbers is ☐.

Use the numbers shown in the ● activity to complete these statements.

The sum of an even number of odd numbers is ☐.

The sum of an odd number of odd numbers is ☐.

At the cinema

Work out the answers to these word problems.
Show all your workings.

a My ticket to get into the cinema costs £5.40 and my drink and ice-cream cost £2.62. How much did I spend altogether?

b 372 people went to the 3 o'clock showing of the film and 594 went to the 6 o'clock showing. How many people went altogether?

c 1265 people went to the cinema on Monday and 1782 went on Tuesday. How many people went altogether?

d I went to the cinema with £8.60. I spent £6.43. How much do I have left?

e At one film, 864 ice-creams were sold. 371 were chocolate. How many were other flavours?

f At one film 28·6 litres of orange juice was drunk and 16·9 litres of water. How much was drunk altogether?

 1 Work out the answers to these word problems. Show all your workings.

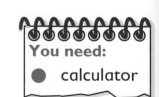
You need:
● calculator

a The cinema can seat 1860 people. It is full for three films. How many people saw these films?

b In a week, 1472 chocolate, 2642 vanilla and 3108 strawberry ice-creams were sold. How many ice-creams were sold that week?

c The total spent on popcorn on Monday came to £68.24 and £29.38 on Tuesday. **i** How much was spent altogether? **ii** What was the difference between the two amounts?

d The total spent on fizzy drinks on Monday was £96.17 and £74.83 on Tuesday. **i** What was the difference between the two totals? **ii** What was the total spent altogether?

e At the end of a film everyone was asked if they had enjoyed it. 486 said 'yes', 572 said 'OK' and 194 said 'no'. How many people saw the film?

f On Tuesday 76·5 litres of cola were drunk, and 57·9 litres of lemonade. How much was drunk altogether?

g 2467 people wanted to buy tickets for the first showing of a film. The cinema holds 1860 people. How many people couldn't buy tickets?

2 Now check your answers using a calculator.

Make up four word problems for a friend to work out:
- one adding money
- one subtracting money
- one adding three four-digit numbers
- one with kilograms

In your head

● **Represent a problem by identifying and recording the calculation**

Work out the answers to these word problems in your head. Make jottings if you need to.

a I spent £21 on some shoes and £36 on a jacket. How much did I spend altogether?

b We picked 83 apples from our tree. We gave 37 to our neighbours. How many apples did we have left?

c 158 people bought books from the book shop on Saturday. Credit cards were used by 79 of them and the rest paid cash. How many people paid with cash?

d I went to the market with £24. I came back with £13. How much did I spend?

e I weigh 37 kg and my dad weighs 82 kg. What is our total weight?

f The car park has 271 cars. At midday 72 more arrive. How many cars are there altogether?

Work out the answers to these word problems in your head. Make jottings if you need to.

a I am thinking of a number. If I subtract 57 and then subtract 38 I am left with 27. What is the number?

b I have £78. I spend £25 in one shop and some more money in another shop. I have £17 left. How much do I spend in the second shop?

c I am thinking of a number. If I add 36 to it and then 48 I get 97.
What number did I start with?

d Three buses arrive at the museum. At the bus stop 259 people get off the three buses.
There were 89 on the first bus and 97 on the second bus. How many were there on
the third bus?

e I am thinking of a number. I subtract 198 and then add 51 and I get 99. What number
am I thinking of?

f Steve has just got the results of his three maths
tests. His total score was 86. He scored 24 in
the first test and his scores in the other two
tests had a difference of 2. What did he score
in the other two tests?

g I am thinking of a number. If I add 62 and 39,
then subtract 17 I get 96. What number am I
thinking of?

h The school has raised £871. The parents raised
£102. Class 5 sponsored silence raised £64. The
rest came from the school fair. How much was
raised at the fair?

What two consecutive two-digit numbers have been
added together to make these totals?

| **a** 47 | **b** 77 | **c** 93 | **d** 131 | **e** 137 |
| **f** 165 | **g** 187 | **h** 171 | **i** 189 | **j** 153 |

Order of operations

- **Begin to use brackets**
- **Recall multiplication facts up to 10 x 10 and the relating division facts**

- Draw a table like the one below.
- Write the number sentence in the first column.
- Decide which order to complete the calculations.
- Write the calculations in the order you do them.
- Write the answer.

Number sentence	First calculation	Next calculation	Answer
3 + 6 × 5	6 × 5 = 30	30 + 3 = 33	33

Remember

Always divide or multiply before you add or subtract unless there are (BRACKETS).
If there are brackets, do what is inside the brackets FIRST!

a 4 × (3 + 5)

b 4 × 3 + 5

c 12 + 16 ÷ 4

d (25 ÷ 5) × 3

e (32 − 8) ÷ 3

f 10 + 30 ÷ 3

g 3 × 3 × 2

h (18 ÷ 2) × 7

i 36 ÷ (6 × 2)

j 36 ÷ 6 × 2

Class 5 worked out how many different answers they could get from the number sentence.

2 + 8 × 4 + 5 = ☐

2 + (8 × 4) + 5 = 2 + 32 + 5 = 39
(2 + 8) × 4 + 5 = 10 × 4 + 5 = 45
2 + 8 × (4 + 5) = 2 + 72 = 74
(2 + 8) × (4 + 5) = 10 × 9 = 90

1 How many different answers can you get from these calculations?
(You can put brackets around any calculation – remember to calculate what is inside the brackets first!)

a 36 ÷ 6 × 2 + 1

b 7 × 8 ÷ 4 × 2

c 3 × 4 ÷ 2 + 4

d 15 − 5 × 4 + 6

e 10 + 10 − 5 × 3

f 6 × 4 − 3 × 6

g 10 + 10 − 5 × 3

h 7 × 4 + 2 × 3

i 40 ÷ 4 + 4 × 6

j 7 × 4 + 2 × 3

k 32 ÷ 8 × 4 + 5

l 9 × 5 + 15 ÷ 3

2 Draw a table like the one below.

Number sentence	First calculation	Second calculation	Next calculation	Answer
(20 ÷ 4) × 3 − 5	20 ÷ 4 = 5	5 × 3 = 15	15 − 5 = 10	10

● Write the number sentence in the first column.
● Decide which order to complete the calculations.
● Write the calculations in the order you do them.
● Write the answer.

a 2 × 5 + 3 × 9   b 72 ÷ 9 + 4 × 3   c 56 ÷ (8 − 1) × 7   d (33 + 3) ÷ 4 − 3

e 9 × 9 − 10 × 3   f (9 × 9) − 10 + 1   g (48 − 8) ÷ 4 × 2   h 48 − (8 ÷ 4) × 2

i 48 − 8 ÷ (4 × 2)   j 16 + (5 × 2) × 6   k 6 × 4 + 8 × 7   l 36 ÷ (16 − 7) − 4

1 Copy and complete these number sentences.

a (3 × 4) + ☐ = 27

b (5 × 5) − ☐ = 14

c 4 × 3 × 2 + ☐ = 25

d 5 × ☐ + 2 × 3 = 36

e 24 ÷ ☐ × 4 × 2 = 24

f 16 × ☐ ÷ 4 + 4 = 8

g (25 − ☐) × 3 × 2 = 120

h 42 ÷ (☐ × 3) × 12 = 24

i 3 × 9 + 6 × ☐ = 81

j ☐ ÷ 5 + 7 × 9 = 70

2 Use any combinations of these symbols to make the number sentences below true.

(+) (−) (×) (÷)

a 16 ☐ 4 ☐ 3 ☐ 4 = 16

b 24 ☐ 2 ☐ 6 ☐ 3 = 24

c 8 ☐ 4 ☐ 2 ☐ 1 = 1

d (6 ☐ 3) ☐ (6 ☐ 3) = 18

e (15 ☐ 9) ☐ (15 ☐ 9) = 30

f (12 ☐ 2 ☐ 2) ☐ 6 = 8

g (8 ☐ 7) ☐ 3 ☐ 9 = 5

h 8 ☐ (6 ☐ 4) ☐ 8 = 4

Doubling and halving whole numbers

● **Double and halve whole numbers**

1 Double each number.

2 Halve each number.

87
53
82
79
96
65
61
24
38
56

194
156
140
178
190
186
124
132
138
-150

Example

61 + 61 = 122

Example

$\frac{1}{2} \times 124 = 62$

540
920
810
690
907
350
718
750
342
430
313
220
970
1000
780
406
217
160
330

● Double each number.

Example

130 × 2 = 260

● Halve each number.

Example

130 ÷ 2 = 65

3 Copy and complete the diagrams to show that halving is the inverse of doubling.

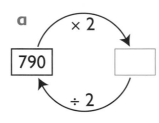
a
× 2
790 [ ]
÷ 2

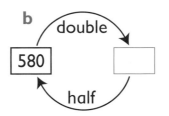
b
double
580 [ ]
half

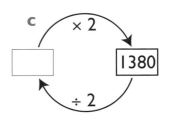
c
× 2
[ ] 1380
÷ 2

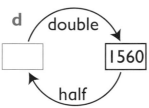
d
double
[ ] 1560
half

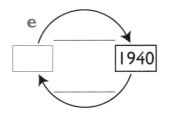
e
[ ] 1940

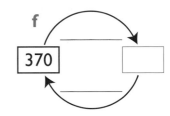
f
370 [ ]

Play the doubles game!

A game for 2 players.

● Place the number cards face down in a pile.

● Turn over the top card. Both players write the number down.

● Start the minute timer. Double the number and keep doubling your answer until the minute is up.

● Compare your answers. The player with the most correct numbers scores 1 point.

● The first player to reach 10 points is the winner.

You need:

● about 20 two-digit number cards

● a 1-minute timer

● paper and pencil

Decimal doubles and halves

 1 Double each of these decimals.

a	5·2	f	0·11
b	3·1	g	0·45
c	7·3	h	0·92
d	2·5	i	0·73
e	8·4	j	0·34

Example

$2·3 × 2$

$2·0 × 2 = 4$	or	$2·3 × 10 = 23$
$0·3 × 2 = 0·6$		$23 × 2 = 46$
$4 + 0·6 = 4·6$		$46 ÷ 10 = 4·6$

2 Halve each of these decimals.

a	8·6	f	0·24
b	6·4	g	0·12
c	10·2	h	0·28
d	2·6	i	0·46
e	4·8	j	0·16

Example

$6·8 ÷ 2$

$6·0 ÷ 2 = 3$	or	$6·8 × 10 = 68$
$0·8 ÷ 2 = 0·4$		$68 ÷ 2 = 34$
$3 + 0·4 = 3·4$		$34 ÷ 10 = 3·4$

 1 Double each of these decimals.

a	3·6	f	2·9
b	5·8	g	9·7
c	8·6	h	7·6
d	4·7	i	10·8
e	6·5	j	1·7

2 Halve each of these decimals.

a	9·7	f	1·5
b	8·3	g	6·8
c	5·5	h	4·6
d	3·9	i	10·7
e	2·7	j	7·3

● Double each of these decimals.

a 0·56
b 0·37
c 0·89
d 0·48
e 0·26

f 0·17
g 0·65
h 0·96
i 0·78
j 0·59

4 Halve each of these decimals.

a 0·64
b 0·88
c 0·22
d 0·46
e 0·68

f 0·34
g 0·76
h 0·52
i 0·96
j 0·78

Play the halving game!

Work with a partner.

● Place the number cards face down in a pile.
● Turn over the top card. Both players write the number down.
● Halve the number and keep halving your answer until you reach a decimal with 2 decimal places.
● Compare your answers. If necessary, check your answers using a calculator.
● The player with more correct numbers scores 1 point.
● The first player to reach 10 points is the winner.
● Can you keep halving until you reach a decimal with 3 decimal places?

You need:

● about 20 two-digit number cards, e.g. 45, 63, 72...
● paper and pencil
● calculator (for checking)

45, 22·5, 11·25

45

Sorting numbers by divisibility

 In each of the four sets of multiples below, there is one number that does not belong. Which numbers are these?

1 Find the numbers that belong. Which set of multiples do they belong to?

2 Write a rule for each set of multiples.

3 Write a divisibility rule for each set of numbers.

4 Write the number that does not belong.

600   2900   900   4500   1700
    450   3100   8200

a Multiples of ☐

● The multiples of ☐ end in ☐

● A number is divisible by ☐ if ☐

740   265   4150   1395   520
    675   626   435

b Multiples of ☐

● The multiples of ☐ end in ☐

● A number is divisible by ☐ if ☐

464   966   7852   268   4324
1208   5712   384

c Multiples of ☐

● The multiples of ☐ end in ☐

● A number is divisible by ☐ if ☐

330   720   4570   1490   3260
    5620   141   480

d Multiples of ☐

● The multiples of ☐ end in ☐

● A number is divisible by ☐ if ☐

 Sort the numbers into the correct container.
Use the 'divisible by' labels to help you.
(Some numbers may go into more than 1 container.)

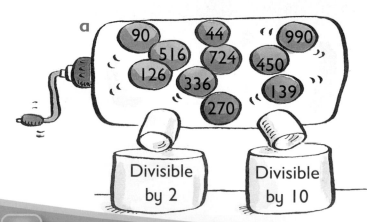

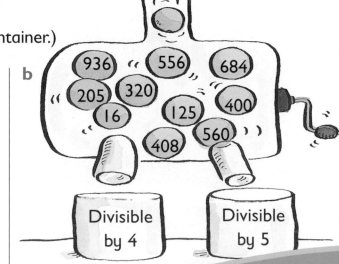

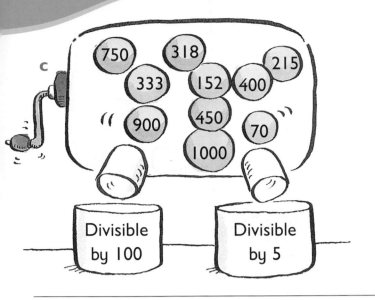

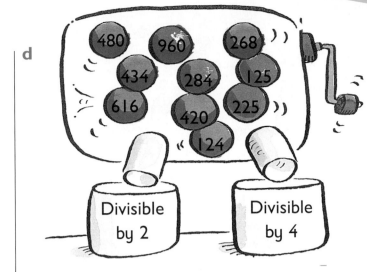

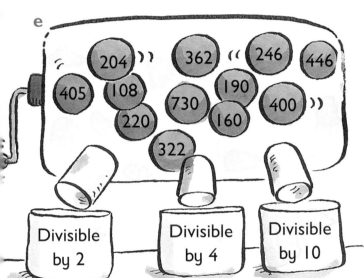

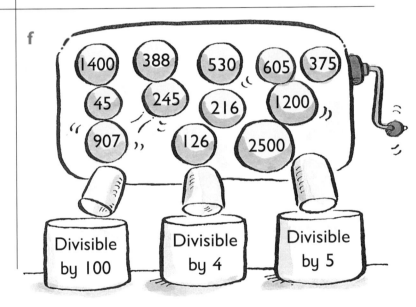

Use your knowledge of divisibility tests to answer these questions.

a Leap years occur every four years. Was the year 1352 a leap year? How do you know?

b The Olympic Games are held in leap years. In what years were the Olympics held in the decade 1960–1970? 1990–2000? How do you know?

c In one African country, presidential elections are held roughly every five years. If there was an election in the year 2000, when would the next four elections occur? How do you know?

d A century equals 100 years. Write the centuries that will occur this millennium. How do you know?

e A decade equals ten years. Write the decades between the years 1900 and 2000. How do you know?

f A shoe company produced 45 678 shoes. Will each shoe have a pair? How do you know?

Counting in steps of 25

Recognise and extend number sequences

 Find your way up or down each set of stairs by counting in 25s.

Example

200, 225, 250, 275

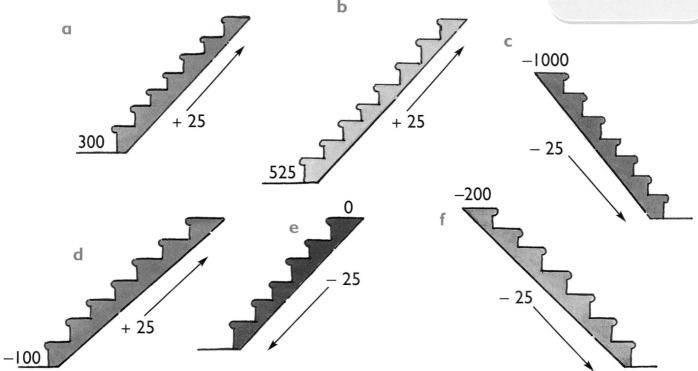

a

300   + 25

b

525   + 25

c

−1000

− 25

d

−100   + 25

e

0

− 25

f

−200

− 25

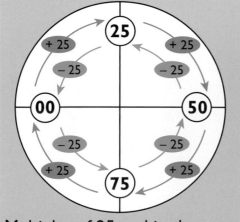

Look at the cycle.

● Start anywhere on the cycle.

● Follow the arrows around the number of 25s you need.

● Your answer will always have one of the endings shown on the cycle.

Multiples of 25 end in the repeated pattern 25, 50, 75, 00

Adding multiples of 25 to multiples of 25 is EASY!

Example

Start at 225
Add 50 (two lots of 25)
Finish at 275

Start at 475
Add 75 (three lots of 25)
Finish at 550

● Copy and complete the table using the cycle to help you.

Start	Add/subtract	Finish	Number sentence
175	+ 50	225	175 + 50 = 225
525	+ two lots of 25		
700	+ 75		
975	+ 25		
− 250	+ three lots of 25		
825	− 50		
− 475	+ 75		
300	− 25		
250	− 75		
	+ 50	−325	
	− 25	450	
	− 75	225	
	+ 100	−325	

2 Copy and complete these calculations.

a 675 + 50 = ☐   b −150 + 75 = ☐   c 925 − 50 = ☐

d −350 + 25 = ☐   e 725 + 75 = ☐   f − 600 + 25 = ☐

g 500 − 75 = ☐   h − 475 + 50 = ☐   i 1000 − 75 = ☐

Copy and complete each table.

	+50	−25	+100	−75
675				
925				
−375				
700				
−550				
−875				

	+25	−50	+75	−100
−950				
−1000				
1000				
475				
−850				

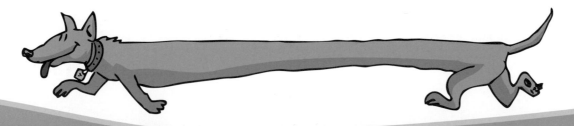

All sorts of triangles

- Say whether a triangle is isosceles, equilateral or scalene, using criteria such as equal sides, equal angles
- Investigate a general statement and say whether examples are true or false

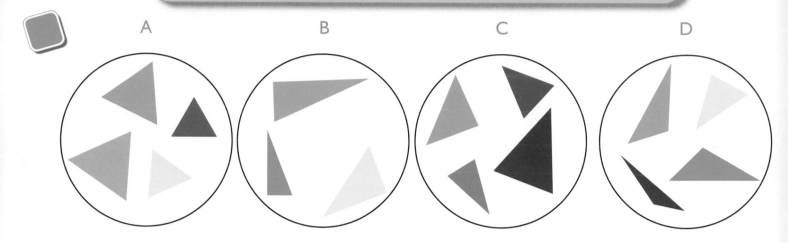

A   B   C   D

Look at sets of triangles A to D. Label each set:
scalene, right-angled, equilateral or isoceles.

1 Statement: *A triangle can be right-angled and isosceles.*

Copy these right angles onto squared paper.
Draw one more line to make a right-angled triangle.

You need:
- 1 cm squared paper
- ruler

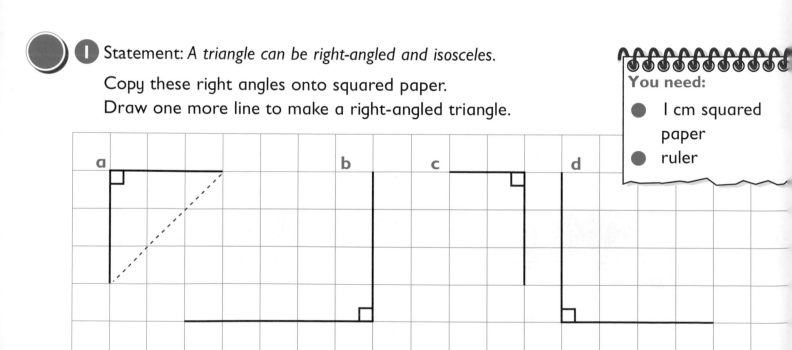

Now check if the statement is true or false.

44

● Statement: *A triangle can be right-angled and scalene.*

In the same way, draw these angles on squared paper and complete the triangle.

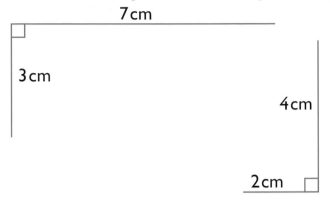

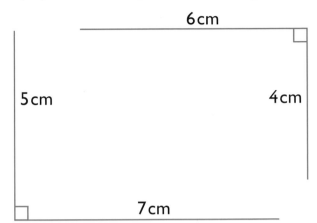

Is the statement true or false?

③ Look at these Venn diagrams.
Decide which one is correct. Give a reason for your answer.

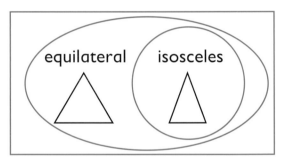

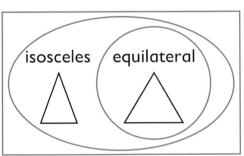

Write the family to which each of these triangle shapes belongs.

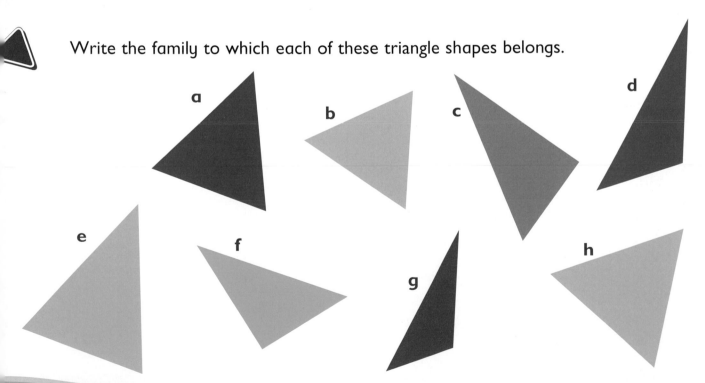

Symmetry in triangles

- **Say whether a triangle has line symmetry or not**
- **Identify triangles using properties such as equal sides, equal angles or a right angle**

Use the Decision tree to sort these six triangles.
Write the name of the triangle for each end branch.
The first one is done for you.

You need:
- ruler

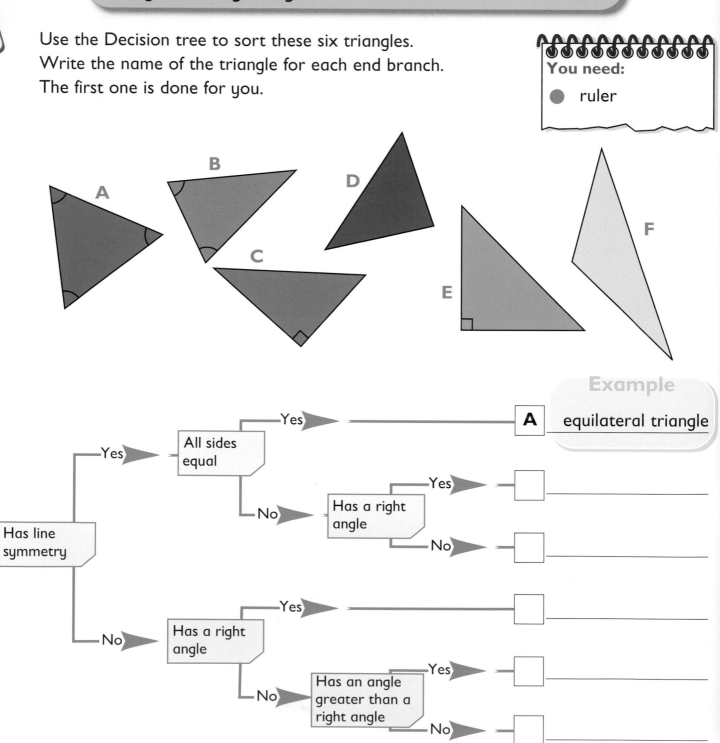

Has line symmetry

Yes → All sides equal
- Yes → **A** equilateral triangle *(Example)*
- No → Has a right angle
  - Yes → ☐
  - No → ☐

No → Has a right angle
- Yes → ☐
- No → Has an angle greater than a right angle
  - Yes → ☐
  - No → ☐

1 Copy this square onto square dot paper. Draw straight lines to make 3 triangles. Cut out the triangles. Check by folding to find if each triangle has line symmetry.

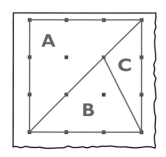

You need:
- 1 cm squared dot paper
- ruler
- scissors

2 Copy and complete this table.

Triangle	Type	has line symmetry
A		
B		
C		

3 Copy, cut out, fold and record these squares and rectangles in the same way.

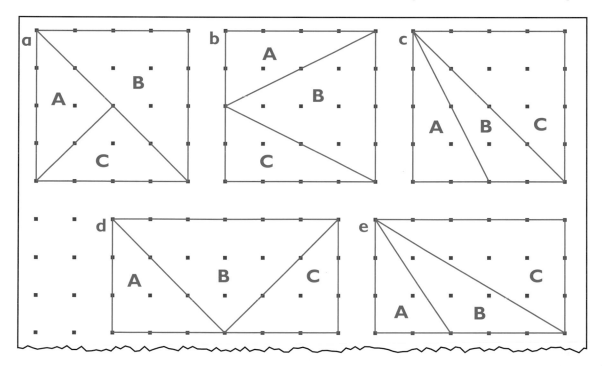

 Copy one of the squares or rectangles from question **2** of the ⬤ activity onto square dot paper. Find ways you can make 4 triangles in the shape. Make a table and record your findings.

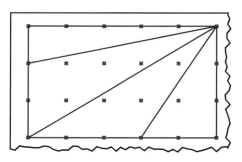

You need:
- 1 cm square dot paper
- ruler
- protractor

47

Reflective symmetry in regular polygons

● **Recognise reflective symmetry in regular polygons**

Draw each irregular quadrilateral on squared paper and cut out the shape.
Test each shape for symmetry by using a mirror and by folding.
Draw the lines of symmetry with a ruler.

You need:
● 1 cm squared paper
● scissors
● ruler
● mirror

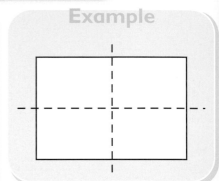

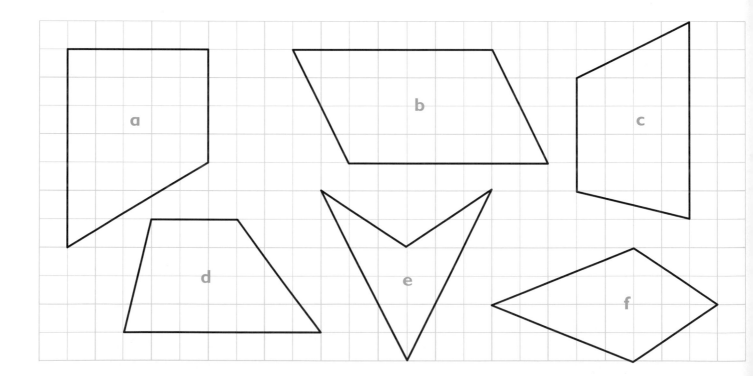

1 a Draw round the templates and cut out the six regular polygons.

b By folding only, find and draw the axes of symmetry in each polygon.

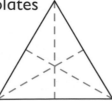

equilateral triangle

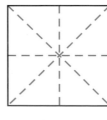

square

You need:
● templates of 3- to 8-sided regular polygons
● scissors ● ruler

c Copy and complete the table.

Regular polygon	Number of		
	equal sides	equal angles	lines of symmetry
Equilateral triangle	3	3	3
Square			
Pentagon			
Hexagon			
Heptagon			
Octagon			

2 Use your findings in the table above to complete this table..

Regular polygon	Number of		
	equal sides	equal angles	lines of symmetry
9-sided			
10-sided			
11-sided			
12-sided			

3 Copy and complete this general statement:

The number of lines of symmetry in a regular polygon is equal to ...

If you add different regular polygons together to make a pattern, will you change the number of axes of symmetry of the regular polygon at its centre? Investigate.

You need:

● templates of 3- to 8-sided regular polygons

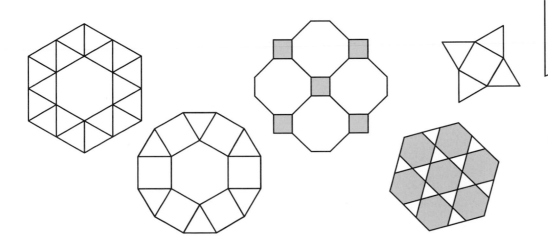

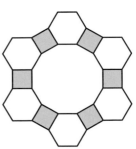

Perpendicular and parallel lines

 For each arrow in the picture, decide whether the **thick** lines are perpendicular or parallel.

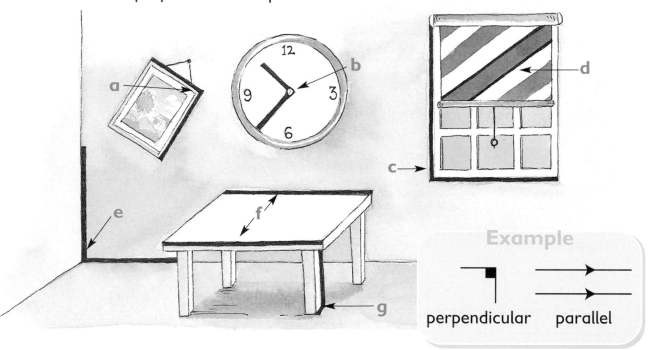

Example

perpendicular   parallel

 **1** This is a drawing of a football pitch. The corners are marked A, B, C and D.

Copy and complete.

a Side AB is parallel to side ☐.

b Side AD is parallel to side ☐.

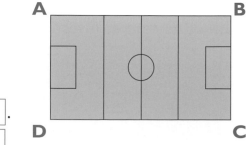

You need:
- 1 cm squared paper
- ruler

2 Helen made a drawing of her house.

a Name 2 pairs of perpendicular lines.

b Name 1 pair of parallel lines.

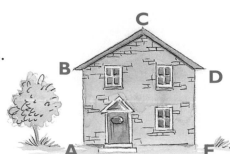

Draw these shapes on squared paper.

a Mark all the parallel lines in both shapes.

b Copy and complete.

The hexagon has ☐ pairs of parallel lines.

The octagon has ☐ pairs of parallel lines.

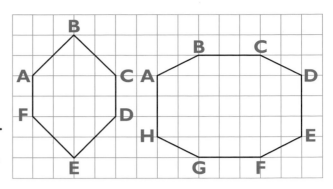

c In the hexagon, draw lines from A to C and from F to D.
Name the shape ACDF and mark its parallel and perpendicular sides.

4 The cube and the square-based pyramid are on a horizontal table.

Which shape has sides which are perpendicular to the table?

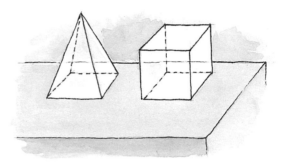

5 Look at the green lines in these drawings. Are the lines parallel? Check with a ruler.

a

b

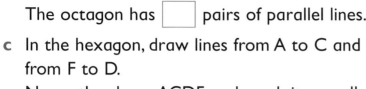

During the American Civil War, Union soldiers used the pig pen code to send secret messages.

1 Can you crack the code to work out this message?

ABC	DEF	GHI
JKL	MNO	PQR
STU	VWX	YZ

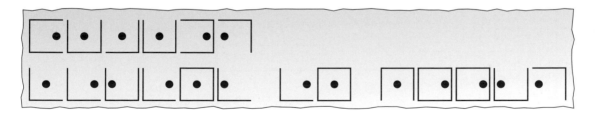

2 Using the pig pen code, write a message to a friend.

Reflecting 2-D shapes

● **Recognise where a shape will be after reflection in a mirror line parallel to one side**

For each word decide whether the reflections are true or false. Use your mirror to check.

You need:
● mirror

Example

TIM
MIT *true*

a

ANDY
∀NDY

b

TAXI TAXI

c

HANNAH HANNAH

d

BETH HT3B

e

f

g

Copy each shape and dotted mirror line on to squared paper. Using the mirror line, find and draw the reflected shape.

You need:
● 1 cm squared paper
● ruler

Example

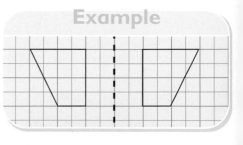

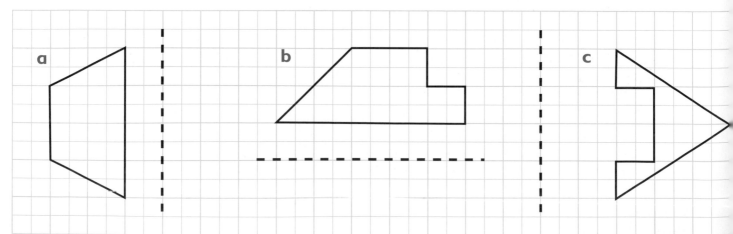

a   **b**   **c**

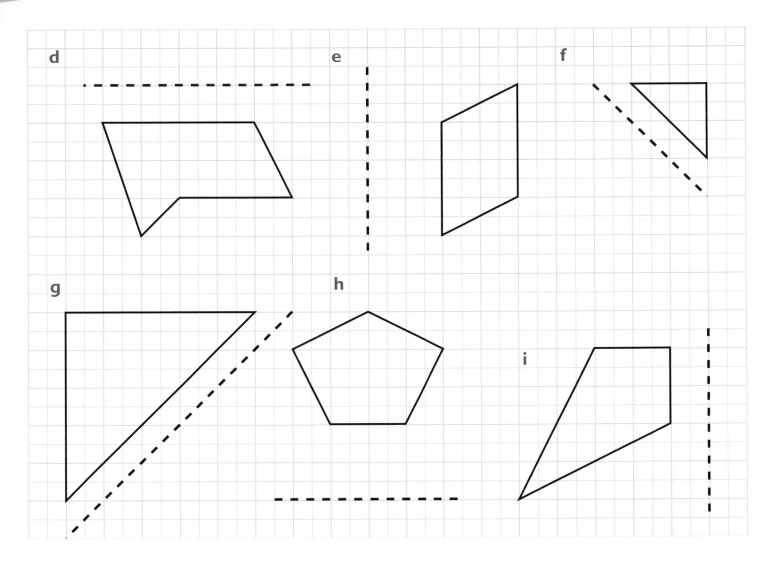

Copy each shape on to squared paper.
Complete the pattern by reflecting the shape in both lines of symmetry.

a
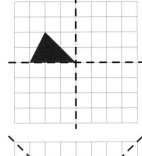

b
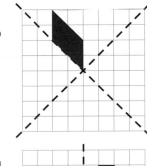

c
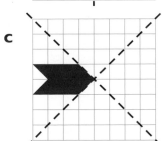

d
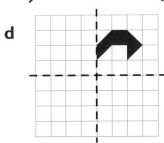

Using standard weights

● **Use, read and write standard metric units of mass**

1 Write these weights in grams.

    a $3\frac{1}{2}$ kg   **b** $4\frac{1}{4}$ kg   **c** $5\frac{3}{4}$ kg

    d $6\frac{1}{10}$ kg   **e** $4\frac{3}{4}$ kg   **f** $6\frac{3}{10}$ kg

> **Example**
>
> $2\frac{1}{2}$ kg = 2000 g + 500 g = 2500 g

2 Write these weights in kilograms and grams.

    a 7470 g   **b** 3860 g   **c** 7070 g

    d 3060 g   **e** 7400 g   **f** 3600 g

> **Example**
>
> 2240 g = 2000 g + 240 g = 2 kg + 240 g

3 Look at the seven standard weights below. You can use each weight more than once to answer these questions.

    a Find a ways to balance 1 kg using: **b** Find a ways to balance 100 g using:

      i 2 weights   **i** 2 weights

      ii 4 weights   **ii** 4 weights

      iii 5 weights   **iii** 5 weights

Standard weights

10 g   20 g   50 g   100 g   200 g   500 g   1000 g

1 Choose 3 standard weights to balance these totals.

    a 650 g   **b** 710 g   **c** 260 g   **d** 1550 g

> **Example**
>
> (500 + 20 + 10) g = 530 g

2 Choose 4 standard weights to balance these totals.

    a 1350 g   **b** 1130 g   **c** 820 g   **d** 730 g   **e** 580 g

3 The table on page 55 shows which standard weights were used to weigh each object. Work out the weight of each object.

    a plastic bowl   **b** dictionary   **c** sports bag   **d** pair of trainers

Object	Standard weights used						
	1000 g	**500 g**	**200 g**	**100 g**	**50 g**	**20 g**	**10 g**
a			2		1		1
b		1	2		1	2	
c	2	1		3		4	
d		1	2		2		4

4 Look at the standard weights on page 54.
Make the pans balance by adding the fewest number of weights.

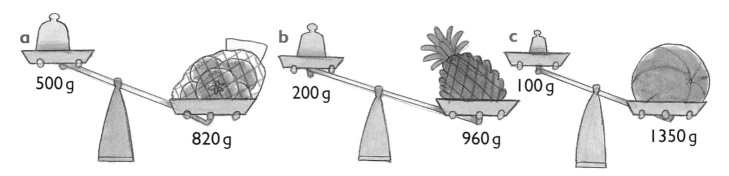

Look at the weights on the balance scales.
Work out the weight of each piece of fruit.

a

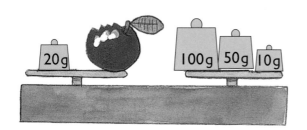

b

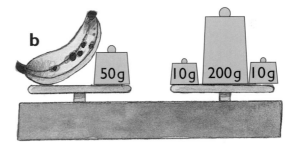

c

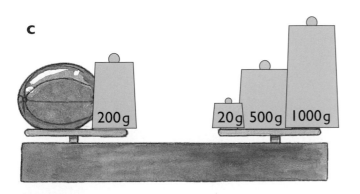

d

Using scales

- Record estimates and readings from scales to a suitable degree of accuracy
- Suggest suitable units and measuring equipment to estimate or measure mass

     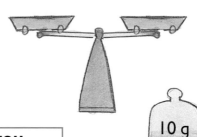

Amount of wool used to knit each soft toy			
ball	**kitten**	**poodle**	**penguin**
15 g blue	30 g black	35 g white	30 g white
15 g white	5 g blue	40 g black	30 g black
			5 g gold

1 Jean brought to school some soft toys that her Gran had knitted. Write the weights Jean would use to balance the scales for each soft toy.

2 List the soft toys in order beginning with the heaviest.

 1 Write the weight in grams shown by each scale.

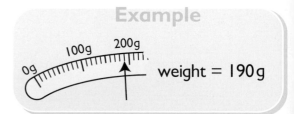

weight = 190 g

a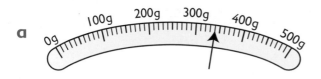

b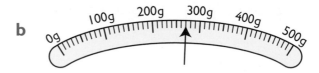

c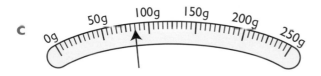

d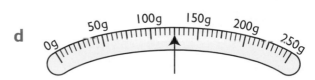

2 Write the weight in kilograms and grams shown by each scale.

a
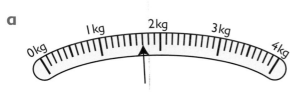

b

c
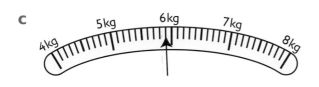

d
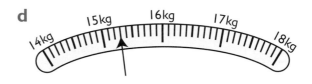

3 For each object, state whether you would use grams or kilograms to record its weight.

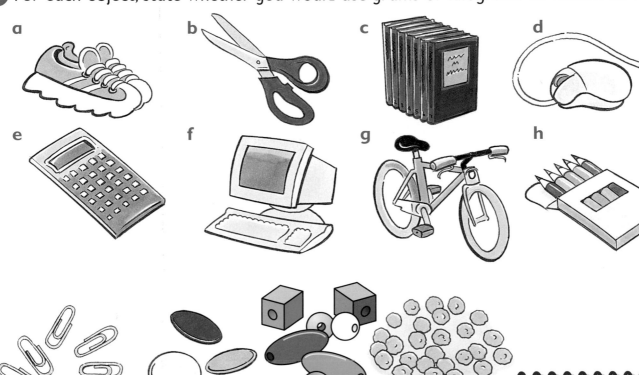

a

b

c

d

e

f

g

h

paper clips   plastic counters   beads   dried peas

1 Choose one of the above sets of objects for weighing.
Find a way to work out about how many of your objects will balance 1 kg.

2 Write down what you did.

3 Repeat for a second set of small objects.

You need:
- some small objects
- one each of these weights: 10 g, 20 g and 50 g
- balance scales

Rounding weights

- Record estimates and readings from scales to a suitable degree of accuracy
- Use all four operations to solve simple word problems using one or more steps

Round these weights to the nearest whole kilogram.
Copy and complete the table.

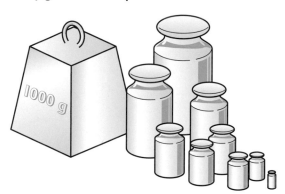

Weight	Rounded to nearest whole kg
5·7 kg	6 kg
2·4 kg	
2·8 kg	
4·2 kg	
4·8 kg	
8·2 kg	
8·4 kg	

1 Using the digits 4, 6 and 8, place each digit in a box to make six different weights.

| 4 | 6 | 8 |

| | . | | | kg |

Example

| 6 | · | 4 | 8 | kg |

2 Copy and complete this table.
Using the 6 different weights from question **1**, round each weight:

a to the nearest tenth of a kilogram
b to the nearest whole kilogram

Weight	Rounded to nearest	
	tenth of a kg	whole kg
6·48 kg	6·5 kg	6 kg

3 Each of these scales shows the weight of a pack of ten books.

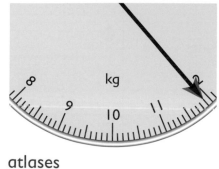

atlases

readers

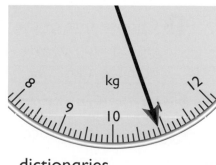

dictionaries

58

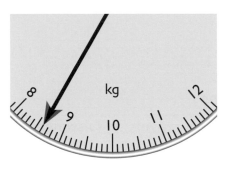
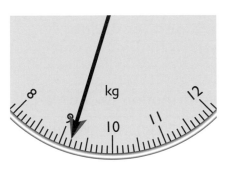
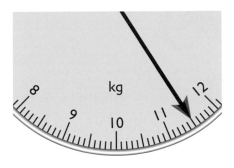

workbooks   textbooks   history books

a Round the weight of each pack to the nearest whole kilogram.

b For each pack, find the weight of 1 book.

c What is the total weight of the pack of atlases and readers?

d How much heavier is the pack of history books than the textbooks?

e Hill Street Primary has ordered 30 dictionaries. What is the total weight of their order?

> **Example**
>
> 11·9 kg → 12 kg
> 11·9 kg ÷ 10 = ?

 1 A boy and his sister took it in turns to stand on a weighing machine with their pet dog.

The brother and sister together weighed 85 kg.
The boy and the dog weighed 60·5 kg.
The girl and the dog weighed 49·5 kg.
Find the weight in kilograms of

a the brother

b the sister

c their pet dog

2 Three collie puppies together weigh 8·6 kg.
Harris is 0·3 kg heavier than Jura.
Jura is 100 g heavier than Lewis.
What does each puppy weigh?

Personal databases

- **Find the mode of a set of data**
- **Organise data to find out about a subject**

This database contains information about Maria's friends.

- Copy the database.
- Add your own name.

Name	Way of travelling to school	Time to travel to school (minutes)	Distance travelled to school (km)
Tara	bus	20	2
Eddie	bus	15	$1\frac{1}{2}$
Jane	cycle	10	1
Leroy	car	15	2
Mike	walk	5	$\frac{1}{2}$
Paula	walk	10	$\frac{1}{2}$
Shane	bus	15	2

1 a What is the longest travel time?

b Who lives $\frac{1}{2}$ km from school?

c How does Leroy travel to school?

d What is the most common way of travelling to school?

e What is the most common distance travelled? What is this number called?

f What is the mode for the time taken to travel to school?

g How many children travel for longer than 10 minutes?

2 Write how you travel to school, how long it takes and how far you travel.

These tables show children's test scores.

Mental maths test scores			
Anila	9	Iris	6
Chris	8	Gary	8
Kate	6	Fay	6
Jim	5	Darren	10
Hattie	2	Bella	5

Spelling test scores			
Gary	7	Jim	8
Hattie	10	Iris	3
Bella	7	Darren	4
Fay	6	Kate	7
Chris	10	Anila	8

1 Copy and complete this database.

Name	Mental maths test score	Spelling test score
Anila	9	8
Bella		

a Which children scored 8 in the spelling test?

b How many children scored above 6 in the mental maths test?

c What is the mode for the mental maths test scores?

d What is the mode for the spelling test scores?

e What is the lowest mental maths test score?

f What is the highest spelling test score?

g Which children did better in the spelling test than in the mental maths test?

h Which children scored a total of 12 in both tests?

i Who got the highest total score?

3 a The children had these results the following week.

Mental maths test: 8 4 9 6 2 5 6 7 8 9
Spelling test: 5 9 8 4 8 10 4 6 3 10

Copy and complete the tables. Use the scores for both weeks.

Mental maths test:	
Score	No. of children

Spelling test:	
Score	No. of children

b Find the new mode for the mental test scores.

c Find the new mode for the spelling test scores.

Make a database about famous people from history.

1 Choose ten famous people from an encyclopaedia or history book.

2 Find out their dates of birth and death. Add them to the database.

3 Work out how long they lived. Add this to the database.

a Who lived the longest?

b Who lived the shortest?

c Who was born first?

d Who died last?

e How many people lived longer than 60 years?

You need:

● books containing information about historical figures

Name	Born	Died	Lifespan
Beethoven	1770	1827	57

Football bar line charts

 Work in pairs.

1 Draw this table in your book.

Goals scored	Tally	Matches
0		
1		
2		
3		

2 Each of you roll the dice to give the results of a football match, for example 0–1. Record the goals each team scores in the table. Do this 20 times.

3 Copy and complete this bar line chart.

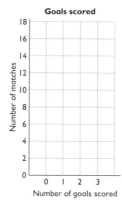

Goals scored

Number of matches (y-axis: 0, 2, 4, 6, 8, 10, 12, 14, 16, 18)

Number of goals scored (x-axis: 0, 1, 2, 3)

4 Use the information in the bar line chart to answer the questions.

a How many teams scored 3 goals?

b How many teams did not score a goal?

c How many teams scored 1 or 2 goals?

d What is the most common number of goals scored?

You need:
● 1 cm squared paper
● ruler
● dice numbered 0, 0, 1, 1, 2, 3 (each)

Work in pairs.

1 Each of you roll the dice to give the results of a football match, for example 2 − 1. Add the goals up. Do this 40 times.

2 Predict the most common total score.

3 Record the total goals scored in this tally chart.

Total goals scored	Tally	Matches
0		
1		
2		
3		

You need:
● blank dice numbered 0, 0, 1, 1, 2, 2 (each)
● 1 cm squared paper
● ruler

2 + 1 = 3
We scored a total of 3 goals.

● Copy and complete this bar line chart.

5 Use the information in the bar line chart to answer the questions.

a How many times was the total number of goals scored 2?

b In how many matches were no goals scored?

c What is the mode? Was your prediction correct?

d In how many matches were less than 2 goals scored?

e In how many matches were 1 or more goals scored?

f Which total number of goals has the lowest frequency?

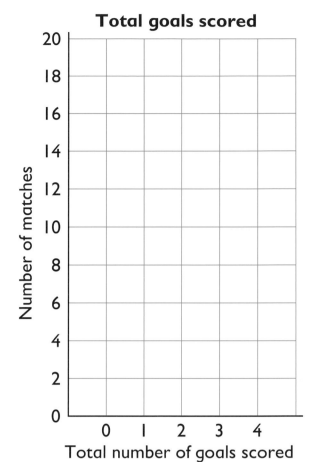

Total goals scored

Number of matches vs Total number of goals scored

▲ Work in pairs.

1 Predict the most common product of rolling two 1-6 dice.

2 Each of you roll the dice. Calculate the product of the numbers. Do this 30 times.

3 Record the products in a tally chart.

4 Draw a bar chart to show your results.

5 Use the information in the bar line chart to answer the questions.

a How many times was the product 4?

b How many times was the product below 3?

c What is the least common product?

d What is the mode?

e How many times was the product 5? Explain your answer.

$2 \times 0 = 0$
The product is 0.

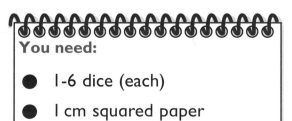

You need:

● 1-6 dice (each)

● 1 cm squared paper

● ruler

Line graphs

● **Draw and interpret line graphs and consider which points do and do not have meaning**

The table shows the cost of 5p stamps.

You need:
● I cm squared paper
● ruler

Number of stamps	Cost (pence)
0	0
1	5
2	10
3	
4	
5	
6	
7	
8	

1 Copy and complete the table.

2 Copy and complete the bar line chart.

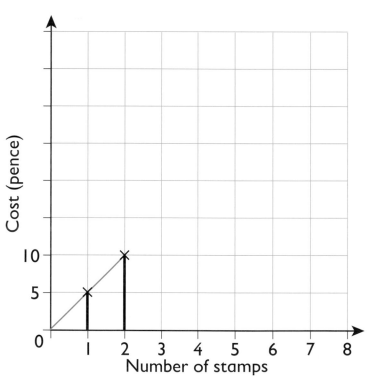

3 Join the tops of the bar lines to make a line graph.

Mark the tops of the bar lines using crosses.

1 Copy and complete the table.

Number of packs	Cost (£)
0	
2	8
4	
6	
8	
10	

You need:
● I cm squared paper
● ruler

● Copy and complete the bar chart.

3 Join the tops of the bar lines to make a line graph.

Mark the tops of the bar lines using crosses.

4 Use your line graph to answer the following questions.

   a How much do 7 packs cost?

   b How many packs could you buy for £12?

5 a Extend your line graph up to 14 packs.

   b How much do 13 packs cost?

6 Which points on the line graph have meaning? Which points do not have meaning?

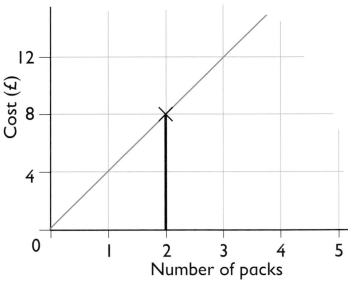

The line graph shows the cost of envelopes.

1 How much do 12 envelopes cost?

2 How many envelopes could you buy for 21p?

3 What is the cost of an envelope?

4 a Does the red cross mean anything?

   b Does the green cross mean anything?

5 a Copy the line graph.

   b Extend the graph up to 20 envelopes.

   c How much do 19 envelopes cost?

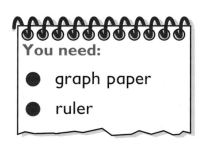

You need:
- graph paper
- ruler

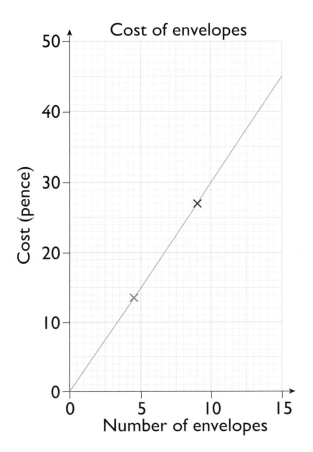

Cost of envelopes

Multiplication line graphs

1 Copy and complete this 4 times table.

$0 \times 4 = 0$
$1 \times 4 =$
$2 \times 4 =$
$3 \times 4 = 12$
$4 \times 4 =$
$5 \times 4 =$
$6 \times 4 =$
$7 \times 4 =$
$8 \times 4 =$
$9 \times 4 =$
$10 \times 4 =$

2 Copy and complete the bar line chart for the 4 times table.

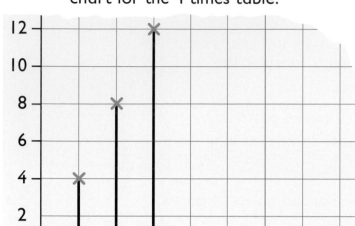

You need:
- squared paper
- ruler
- red and green pencils

3 Mark the top of each bar line using a cross. The points up to 3×4 have been done for you.

4 Join the crosses to make a line graph.

5 Use a red pencil to circle the crosses for these calculations.

a $3 \times 4 = 12$ b $9 \times 4 = 36$ c $7 \times 4 = 28$

6 Use a green pencil to circle the crosses for these calculations.

a $8 \div 4 = 2$ b $32 \div 4 = 8$ c $24 \div 4 = 6$

1 Copy and complete the 6 times table.

$0 \times 6 = 0$
$1 \times 6 =$
$2 \times 6 =$
$3 \times 6 = 18$
$4 \times 6 =$
$5 \times 6 =$
$6 \times 6 =$
$7 \times 6 =$
$8 \times 6 =$
$9 \times 6 =$
$10 \times 6 =$

You need:
- graph paper
- ruler

2 Copy and complete the bar line chart for the 6 times table on page 67.

3 Mark the top of each bar line using a cross.

4 Join the crosses to make a line graph.

Use your graph to answer these calculations.

a $1\frac{1}{2} \times 6 =$

b $8\frac{1}{2} \times 6 =$

c $4\frac{1}{2} \times 6 =$

d $3.5 \times 6 =$

e $9.5 \times 6 =$

f $7.5 \times 6 =$

g $54 \div 6 =$

h $33 \div 6 =$

i $15 \div 6 =$

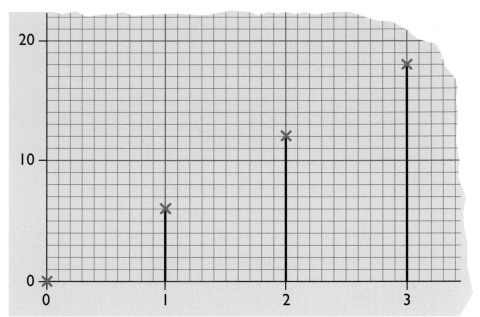

6 Ribbon costs 6p a metre. How much do these children spend altogether? Use your graph to help you answer the questions.

a Marva buys 3·5 m and John buys 7 m.

b Charlie buys 2·5 m, Alec buys 9·5 m and Antoinette buys 5 m.

c Jason buys 6·5 m, Uwana buys 1·5 m and Karen buys 5·5 m.

d Suhail buys 12·5 m.

e Liam buys 14·5 m and Sharon buys 16 m.

1 Draw a line graph for the 7 times table.

2 Use your graph to answer these questions.

a $1\frac{1}{2} \times 7$ b $8\frac{1}{2} \times 7$ c $4\frac{1}{2} \times 7$

d 3.5×7 e 9.6×7 f 7.2×7

3 Estimate the answers to these.

a $40 \div 7$ b $52 \div 7$ c $19 \div 7$

4 Cheese costs £7 per kg. Using the line graph, work out how much these people spend altogether.

a Gavin buys 3·5 kg and Milly buys 2 kg.

b Lana buys 2·8 kg, Francis buys 9·3 kg and Lesley buys 3 kg.

c Kulbir buys 4·6 kg, Lin buys 1·2 kg and Jessie buys 5·7 kg.

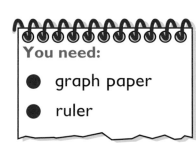

You need:
● graph paper
● ruler

Temperature line graphs

● **Present data using a line graph**

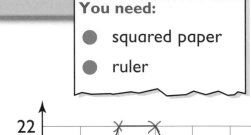

You need:
● squared paper
● ruler

The graph shows the temperature in Paul's bedroom one evening.

1 Copy the line graph.

2 a What was the temperature at 10:00 p.m.?
   b When was the temperature 19 °C?
   c What was the lowest temperature?
   d When was it hottest?
   e When did the temperature fall?
   f Why do you think the temperature fell then?

3 Copy and complete the table.

Time	Temperature (°C)
6 p.m.	
7 p.m.	
8 p.m.	
9 p.m.	
10 p.m.	
11 p.m.	
12 midnight	

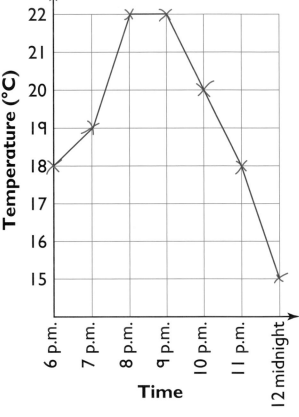

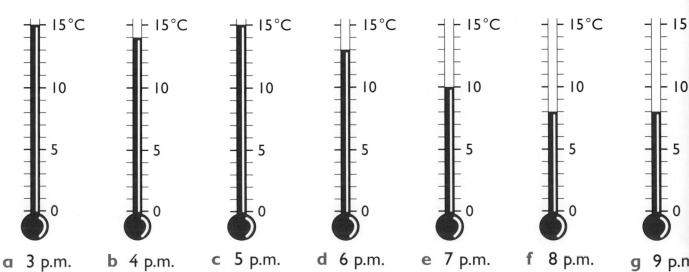

a 3 p.m.   **b** 4 p.m.   **c** 5 p.m.   **d** 6 p.m.   **e** 7 p.m.   **f** 8 p.m.   **g** 9 p.m

Lee read the thermometer outside every hour.

1 Copy and complete her table.

2 Copy and complete the line graph.

Time	Temperature (°C)
3 p.m.	15

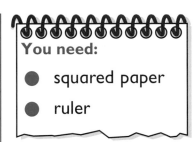

You need:
- squared paper
- ruler

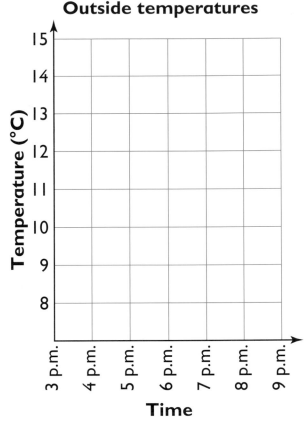

Outside temperatures

3 a When was it coldest outside?

b What was the temperature at 5:00 p.m.?

c At what other time of day was the temperature the same as at 5:00 p.m.?

d How did the temperature change between 5:00 p.m. and 6:00 p.m.?

e When was it colder than 12 °C?

1 The table shows the temperature in Clare's kitchen in one day. Copy and complete the line graph.

You need:
- squared paper
- ruler

Time	Temperature (°C)
10 a.m.	12
11 a.m.	13
12 noon	12
1 p.m.	27
2 p.m.	29
3 p.m.	22
4 p.m.	17

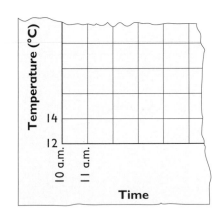

2 a When was the kitchen coldest?

b When was the temperature below 20 °C?

c When do you think Fay did some cooking? Explain your answer.

Chance

● **Describe how likely an event is to happen**

1 Use the phrases in the blue box to describe the likelihood of each of the following events.

a you will break a leg

b you will grow two heads

c you will grow taller

d you will meet Queen Victoria

e you will meet the Prime Minister

f you will see someone tomorrow

g the moon will crash into the Earth

h you will see a meteor next year

i the moon will shine tonight

j you will get older

k you will live longer than your teacher

l you will get younger

2 Copy the scale. Write the letters in question **1** on it.

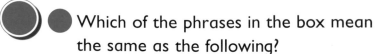

impossible   unlikely   likely   certain

● ● Which of the phrases in the box mean the same as the following?

a unlikely
b impossible
c certain
d likely

high chance   must happen
no chance
low chance
poor chance   good chance   cannot happen

● Copy the scale and then write the letters A to D on it.

| impossible | unlikely | likely | certain |

A

You will come to school at midnight.

B

You will be late for school one day.

C

You will leave school today.

D

You will be off sick all next week.

3 How likely are these to happen?

 a You will be a billionaire.

 b You will be given some money next year.

 c You will write a cheque for over £500.

 d You will own all the money in the world.

impossible   likely
unlikely
certain

4 What are the chances of these happening?

 a You will learn to drive.

 b You will pass your driving test blindfolded.

 c You will see a car next week.

 d You will learn to fly.

no chance
good chance   poor chance
certain

Copy the table. Write three descriptions in each column.

No chance	Poor chance	Good chance	Certain

Take a chance

● **Describe how likely an event is to happen**

Describe the chance of each of the following happening.
Use the words on the right.

certain unlikely likely no chance impossible poor chance good chance

1. I will see a tree fall down on the way home from school.

2. My homework will only take me one minute to do.

3. I will have a snack after school today.

4. I will live to be 50 years old.

5. There will be a power cut today.

6. It will rain tomorrow.

7. I will be a famous singer.

8. If I boil an egg for 10 minutes it will go hard.

Decision spinner

- Play this game in groups.
- Each player writes down four events, one event on each blank card. One must be impossible, one unlikely, one likely, one certain.

- Shuffle the cards and deal out four cards each.

- Each player places their four cards face down in a pile.

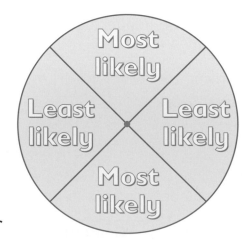

You each need:
● 4 blank cards

Your group needs:
● pencil and paper clip (for the spinner)

- Each player turns over their top card and places it in the middle of the table.

- Everyone in the group then discusses the events on the cards and arranges them in order from the most likely to the least likely.

● Spin the spinner.

● If the Decision Spinner says 'Most likely', the most likely event wins. If the Decision Spinner says 'Least likely', the least likely event wins.

● The winner of the round is the player who placed the winning card face up on the table at the start of the round. They collect all four cards.

● Play continues in this way.

● The player with the most cards at the end is the overall winner.

A game for 2 players.

● Shuffle the set of 0-9 digit cards and place it face down in the middle of the table.

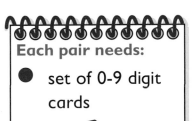

Each pair needs:
● set of 0-9 digit cards

● Take turns to turn over the top card and place it in a row.

● After four cards have been turned over, the next player predicts whether the next card is odd or even, and describes the chance of this happening.

● The card is turned over. The player loses if the prediction is incorrect.

● Play continues until all the cards have been turned over.

Now play this variation.
● Predict whether the next card will be higher or lower than the previous card.

Solve the problems

Work out the answers to these word problems. Choose the method you are going to use. Show all your workings.

a I counted the number of pencils on each table. There were seven on one table, six on another, and eight on the other two tables. How many pencils were there altogether?

b I have been swimming three times this week. On Monday I swam 400 m, on Wednesday 300 m and on Friday 500 m. What was the total number of metres I swam?

c I want to buy a new shirt for £28.76. I have £14.32 so far. How much more do I need?

d On sports day the school made £42.56 from selling cold drinks and £38.23 from selling cakes. How much money was made altogether?

Work out the answers to these word problems. Show all your workings.

a I went out with £21.72 and came home with £3.52. I bought a book for £5.49 and spent the rest on a T-shirt. How much was the T-shirt?

b The school has ordered 1462 new pens: 347 red, 487 blue and the rest black. How many black pens have been ordered?

c I counted how many hours of sleep I have had in the last three months. The total is 723 hours sleep. One month I slept for 248 hours. In the next month I slept for 219 hours. How many hours did I sleep in the third month?

d In three very busy days 1487 people visited an art gallery. 596 came one day, 682 the next. How many came on the third day?

e I measured the length of the playground. The total length was 67·41 m. The grassy area was 19·54 m, the quiet area was 8·13 m. How long was the rest?

Work out the answer to this word problem in your head.

Four girls competed in the long jump on sports day. Helen, who is 9 years old, jumped 5 cm further than Grace. Grace jumped 2 cm less than Rosa, but 2 cm further than Molly. Molly and Grace are cousins.

If Rosa jumped 93 cm how far did the other three girls jump?

Calculate decimals and fractions

● Use a calculator to solve problems including those involving decimals and fractions

1 If you were using your calculator for money questions and you got these answers how would you write them as money?

    a 5·2   **b** 1·8   **c** 8·3

    d 12·7   **e** 11·9   **f** 18·4

2 Explain what the decimal digit represents in question **1**.

3 Work out these word problems using your calculator.
Write down the calculations you use.

    a I spent £13.87 one day and £24.51 the next. How much did I spend altogether?

    b My favourite programme lasts 34 minutes. It was on five times last week. How long did I spend watching it?

    c I had 387 ml of juice left. Mum said I had to share it out equally between myself and my brother and my sister. How much did we get each?

    d Dad said I could have £40 to spend for my birthday. If I spent £28.39 on a new computer game how much did I have left to spend?

1 Use a calculator to work out these decimal calculations.

    a 76·23 + 56·83

    b 89·43 + 72·64

    c 128·4 + 69·3

    d 184·25 + 79·62

    e 23·4 + 71·3 + 82·9

BEEP BEEP

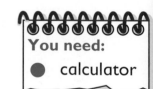

2 Choose one of the calculations from question and check your answer without using the calculator.

3 Use a calculator to work out these fraction calculations. Write down the keys you pressed.

BEEP
BEEP

a $\frac{1}{4}$ of 8·4

b $\frac{1}{3}$ of 11·4

c $\frac{1}{5}$ of 18·5

d $\frac{1}{4}$ of 13·96

e $\frac{1}{6}$ of 27·3

4 Use the calculator to solve the following word problems. Write down the calculations you use.

a I bought three books in a sale for £17.88.
   i   If the full price was £28.93 how much did I save?
   ii If each of the books cost the same, how much did each one cost me?
   iii If I walked past the shop again the following week and all the books were reduced by another quarter, how much more would I have saved?
   iv If, after a week, I had read two of my books, what fraction of the books would I have read?

b I have 522 grams of sweets.
   i   If I share them into 6 equal bags how much will each bag weigh?
   ii If I sell them for 65p a bag, how much will I have?
   iii If I eat 78 grams and my friend eats double that, what will I have left?
   iv If my dad takes $\frac{1}{3}$ of the sweets what will I have left?

If the answer is 89·4, what could the questions be?
Use your calculator to work out 10 possibilities.

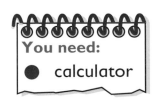

You need:
● calculator

Multiplying and dividing by 10, 100 and 1000

● Use understanding of place value to multiply and divide whole numbers and decimals by 10, 100 or 1000

Larger product wins

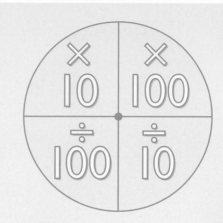

You need:
● pencil and paper
● paper clip

A game for 2 players.
Each player writes down a different two-digit number, e.g. 57 and 83.

One player then spins the spinner, e.g. × 100, and performs this operation on their two-digit number, i.e. 57 × 100 = 5700.

The next player then spins the spinner, e.g. ÷ 10, and performs this operation on their two-digit number, i.e. 83 ÷ 10 = 8·3.

The player with the larger answer wins a point.

The overall winner is the first player to win 10 points.

Play the game again, this time each player writes down a different three-digit number. e.g. 385 and 437.

1 Multiply each of these by 10.

55
605
0·8
0·24

2 Divide each of these by 10.

6
99
652
6·5

Multiply each of these by 100.

53

112

0·2

0·68

Divide each of these by 100.

9

850

5620

4521

5 Multiply each of these by 1000.

13

16

1·2

0·34

6 Divide each of these by 1000.

30

400

8000

6500

Smaller product wins

A game for 2 players.

Each player writes down a different three-digit number. e.g. 648 and 247.

One player then spins the spinner, e.g. × 1000, and performs this operation on their three-digit number, i.e. 648 × 1000 = 648 000.

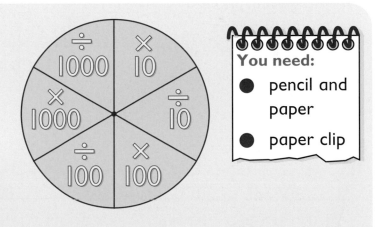

You need:
- pencil and paper
- paper clip

The next player then spins the spinner, e.g. ÷ 100, and performs this operation on their three-digit number, i.e. 247 ÷ 100 = 2·47.

The player with the smaller product wins a point.

The overall winner is the first player to win 10 points.

Play the game again, this time each player writes down a different four-digit number. e.g. 6485 and 4315.

Reviewing multiplication

Use efficient written methods to multiply HTU x U, TU x TU and U.t x U

Example

$246 \times 7 \to 250 \times 7 = 1750$

×	200	40	6
7	1400	280	42

```
 1400
  280
+  42
 1722
    1
```

or

```
  246
×   7
 1400    (200 × 7)
  280    (40 × 7)
   42    (6 × 7)
 1722
    1
```

- Choose one of the numbers from the grid below.
- Then roll the dice.
- Estimate what the product of these two numbers is and write it down.
- Then multiply the two numbers together. Show all your working.
- Your teacher will tell you how many times to do this.

You need:
- 0-9 dice

653	832	253	43
167	314	545	784
946	508	387	498
625	796	862	326

Example

$28 \times 46 \to 30 \times 45 = 1350$

×	20	8
40	800	320
6	120	48

```
  800
  320
  120
+  48
 1288
```

or

```
   28
×  46
 1120    (40 × 28)
  168    (6 × 28)
 1288
```

- Choose two of the numbers from the grid at the top of page 81.
- Estimate what the product of these two numbers is and write it down.
- Then multiply the two numbers together. Show all your working.
- Your teacher will tell you how many times to do this.

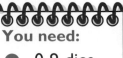

You need:
- 0-9 dice

56	62	45	24
8	18	37	72
93	49	68	53
76	98	39	27

Example

$5 \cdot 3 \times 8 \rightarrow 5 \times 8 = 40$

×	5·0	0·3
8	40	2.4

42·4   or

$$
\begin{array}{r}
5 \cdot 3 \\
\times\ 8 \\
\hline
40 \\
2 \cdot 4 \\
\hline
42 \cdot 4 \\
\end{array}
$$

(5·0 × 8)
(0·3 × 8)

- Choose one of the numbers from the grid on the right.
- Then roll the dice.
- Estimate what the product of these two numbers is and write it down.

6·3	8·8	4·9	2·4
3·7	5·9	7·6	9·8
1·5	2·5	8·2	6·7
4·6	3·2	9·3	7·4

- Then multiply the two numbers together. Show all your working.
- Your teacher will tell you how many times to do this.

ESTIMATING PRODUCTS

A game for 2 players

- One player rolls the dice twice to make a two-digit number.
- The other player rolls the dice twice to make another two-digit number.
- Each player writes down an estimate of the product of these two numbers.
- Each player then calculates the answer and checks to see if they both have the same answer.
- The winner is player with the smaller difference between their estimate and the actual answer.
- Play 10 rounds.
- The overall winner is the player who wins more rounds.

You need:
- 0-9 dice
- pencil and paper each

Key it in

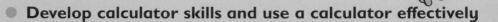

● **Develop calculator skills and use a calculator effectively**

1 Use the calculator to work out these calculations.
Enter the numbers carefully!

You need:
● calculator

a 485 + 67

b £2·79 + £0·81

c 578 + 391

d £5·70 + £2·94

e 617 + 271

f £7·51 − £0·68

g 593 − 81

h £6·42 − £2·9

i 384 − 173

j £75·90 − £21·80

k £16 × 43

l 36 × 21

m 26 × £0·13

n 17 × 33

o 22 × 38

p £2·16 ÷ 8

q 306 ÷ 9

r 294 ÷ 7

s £318 ÷ 6

t 592 ÷ 8

2 Calculator cricket

Play with a partner.

● One person is Player A, the other is Player B.
● Player A chooses a four-digit number, for example 6532,
  enters it into the calculator and writes it down.
● Player A then underlines one of the digits.
● Player B has to say the subtraction calculation to make that
  digit zero.
● Player A then enters
  the calculation into the
  calculator to check the result.
● Repeat the game several times,
  changing roles.

You need:
● calculator
  (per pair)

1 Use the calculator to work out these calculations. Enter the numbers carefully!

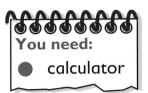
You need:
● calculator

a 4823 + 684

b £75.28 + £9.14

c £8473 + £6.54

d 3819 + 829

e 2674 + 2941

f 7458 − 657

g £86.31 − £7.52

h £68.31 − £4.58

i 7635 − 1579

j 4197 − 2067

k £0.49 × 37

l £0.98 × 62

m £1.57 × 36

n 261 × 75

o 452 × 103

p £57.24 ÷ 36

q 14 736 ÷ 48

r 54 610 ÷ 86

s £243.88 ÷ 91

t £214.24 ÷ 52

Now check your answers with a friend.

2 **Calculator cricket**

You need:
● calculator (per pair)

Play with a partner.
● One person is Player A, the other is Player B.
● Player A chooses a five-digit number, for example 43 578, enters it into the calculator and writes it down.
● Player A then underlines one of the digits.
● Player B has to say the subtraction calculation to make that digit zero.
● Player A then enters the calculation into the calculator to check the result.
● Repeat the game several times, changing roles.

Can you make all the numbers to 20 on your calculator?
You are only allowed to press these keys:

You need:
● calculator
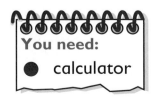

Plotting and constructing

1 a List the co-ordinates of this shape.

b Plot these points on to the first 6 × 6 co-ordinate grid. Join them in a clockwise order to make a shape. (1, 1), (1, 3), (3, 3), (3, 1).

c Write about any patterns you notice.

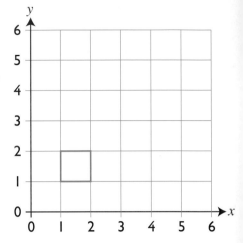

2 Three of the vertices of a square have been plotted.

a Copy these diagrams on to the 2nd and 3rd 6 × 6 co-ordinate grids. Complete the square in each case.

b Write the co-ordinates of the 4th vertex of each square.

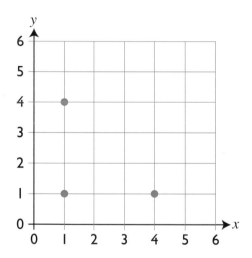

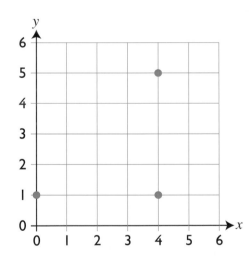

You need:

● RCM 7: 6 × 6 co-ordinate grids

● ruler

1 a Look at the co-ordinate grid at the top of the next page. On your first co-ordinate grid, construct square A drawing sides parallel to the axes.

b List the co-ordinates of the vertices in a clockwise order.

2 Construct 3 more squares, B, C and D, on the first grid making each square a different size and colour.

You need:

● RCM 8: 9 × 9 co-ordinate grids

● set square

● ruler

● colouring materials

3 Three of the vertices of a square are (2, 1), (2, 4) and (5, 4). Construct the square on a 2nd grid. Write the co-ordinates of the 4th vertex.

4 a These points are the co-ordinates of the vertices of a shape.

(1, 5), (2, 5), (4, 3), (2, 1) and (1, 1). Construct the shape on to a 3rd grid. Join the points in a clockwise order. Name the shape you have drawn.

b Repeat as above for this set of co-ordinates. (1, 3), (5, 7), (7, 5) and (3, 1).

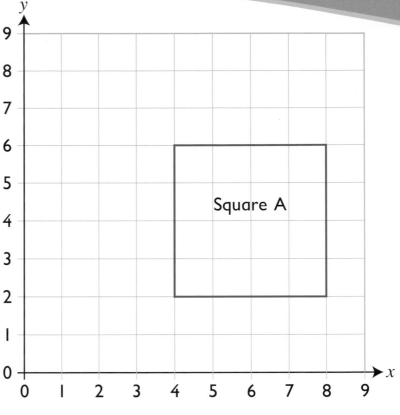

Square A

5 On a further grid, use a ruler and set square to construct:

a A square with sides of 6 cm.

b A rectangle with sides of 4·5 cm and 7 cm.

In these diagrams you can see one side of a square.

a

A (4, 5) B (9, 5)

b

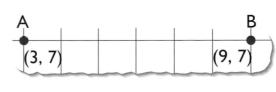

A (3, 7) B (9, 7)

c

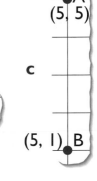

A (5, 5)

(5, 1) B

Write your first choice of co-ordinates for points C and D.
Now find a different set of vertices for each shape.

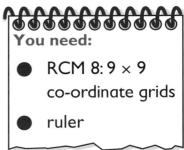

You need:

● RCM 8: 9 × 9 co-ordinate grids

● ruler

Measuring angles

Use a protractor to measure and draw acute and obtuse angles to the nearest 5°

Measure and name these angles. Write the number of degrees.

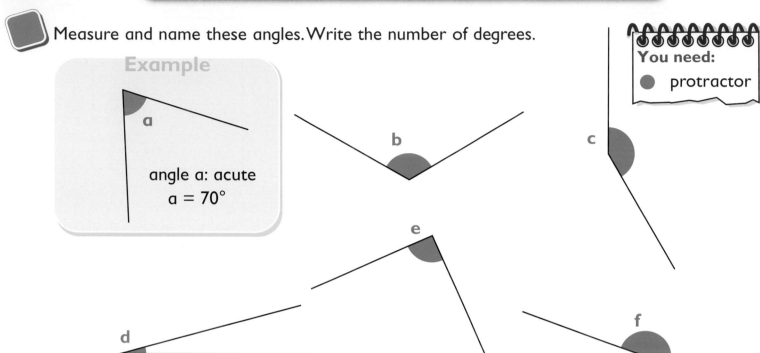

Example

angle a: acute
a = 70°

① Measure these angles to the nearest 5°.

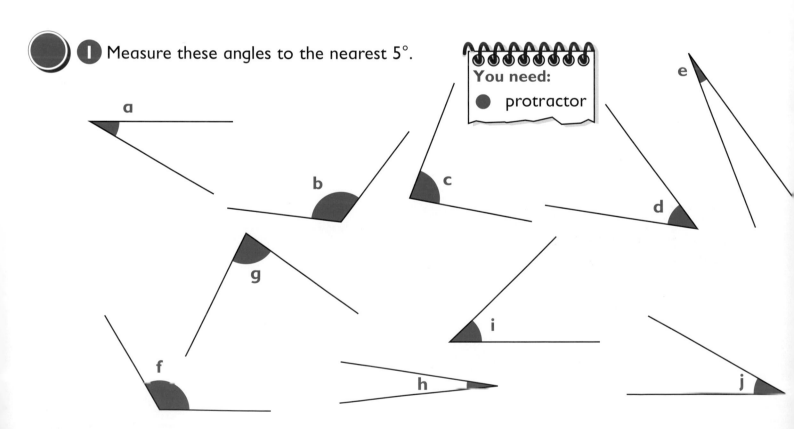

2 List the pairs of angles in question **1** that are the same size.

3 a Measure the marked angles in these shapes. Write the number of degrees.

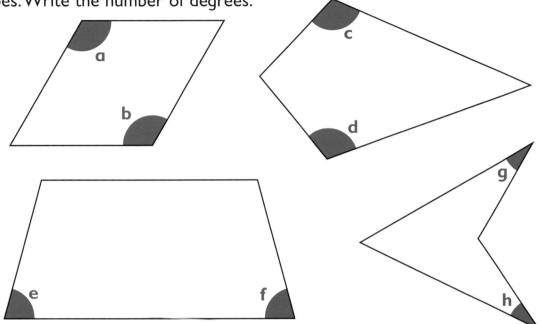

b Write what you notice about your answers.

Angles in an octagon

A game for 2 players.
- Choose an angle. Each player estimates the size of the angle to the nearest 5°.
- Measure the angle.
- The player with the higher score wins.

You need:
- protractor

Scoring	
Exactly right	5 points
Within 5° of the angle size	3 points
Within 10° of the angle size	1 point

- Repeat 7 more times for the remaining vertices.
- The overall winner is the player with more points.

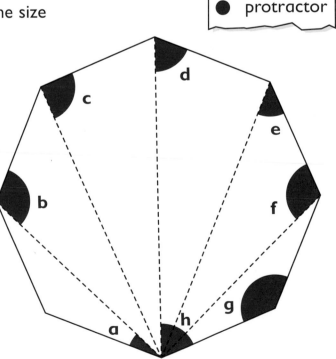

Calculating areas

- **Understand area is measured in square centimetres (cm²)**
- **Use the formula 'length × breadth' for the area of a rectangle**

 1 Find the area of these rectangles. Each square is
1 square centimetre.

Example

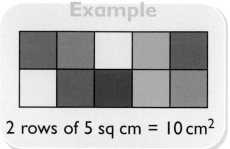

2 rows of 5 sq cm = 10 cm²

a

b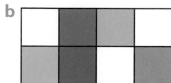

c 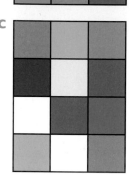   **d** 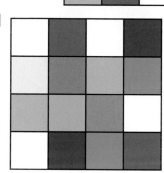   **e**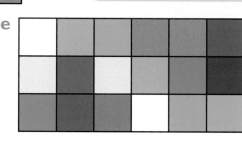

 2 List the rectangles in question **1** in order smallest

1 Find the areas of these rectangles.

Example

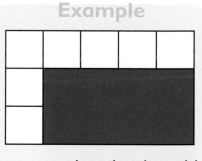

area = length × breadth
= 5 cm × 3 cm
= 15 cm²

a 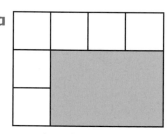   **b**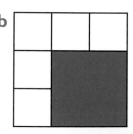

c 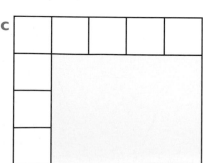   **d** 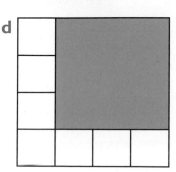   **e** 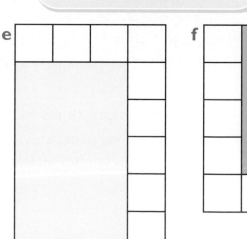   **f**

2 Ellen made a collage with her holiday photographs.

Find the area of each picture.

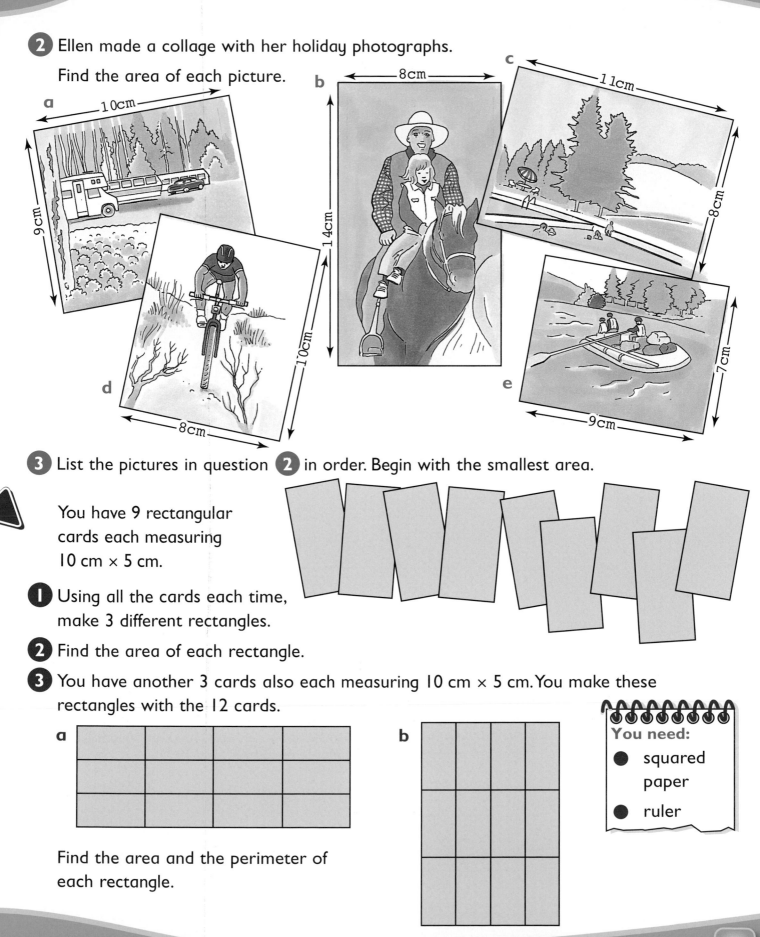

a — 10cm — 9cm

b — 8cm — 14cm

c — 11cm — 8cm

d — 8cm — 10cm

e — 9cm — 7cm

3 List the pictures in question **2** in order. Begin with the smallest area.

You have 9 rectangular cards each measuring 10 cm × 5 cm.

1 Using all the cards each time, make 3 different rectangles.

2 Find the area of each rectangle.

3 You have another 3 cards also each measuring 10 cm × 5 cm. You make these rectangles with the 12 cards.

a

b

Find the area and the perimeter of each rectangle.

You need:
● squared paper
● ruler

Shopping in kilograms

- Convert grams to kilograms using decimals
- Solve problems using mental or written methods

 1 Copy and complete.

250 g = ? kg

Grams (g)	Kilograms (kg) and grams (g)	Fraction (kg)	Decimal (kg)
100 g	0 kg 100 g	$\frac{1}{10}$ kg	0·1 kg
200 g		$\frac{2}{10}$ kg	0·2 kg
400 g			
	0 kg 500 g		
250 g			
	0 kg 750 g		
		kg	1·0 kg

2 Write these weights in three different ways.

a 1200 g   b 2500 g   c 3250 g

pasta – 500 g

butter – 250 g

bread – 800 g

apples – 900 g

tin soup – 400 g

potatoes – 2600 g

flour – 1500 g

cereal – 750 g

sugar – 1000 g

1 Change each food item's weight from grams to kilograms.
Write your answer in decimal form.

2 Calculate the total weight of each of the following pairs of items. Write your answer in grams only and in kilograms using decimals.

a soup and pasta
b sugar and bread
c apples and butter
d flour and pasta

e cereal and flour
f bread and potatoes
g cereal and potatoes
h sugar and flour

> **Example**
>
> flour 1500 g = 1·5 kg
> soup <u> 400 g = 0·4 kg</u>
>   <u>1900 g = 1·9 kg</u>

3 Find the two items which together weigh:

a 1·0 kg   b 1·55 kg   c 2·2 kg   d 4·1 kg

4 Find the total weight of two loaves of bread and two tins of soup.

3-fruit salads

apples
300 g

pears
250 g

cherries
200 g

bananas
400 g

strawberries
250 g

1 Each 3-fruit salad must have apples and two other fruits.

How many different 3-fruit salads can you make with the above fruits?

HINT

Make a list and mark each fruit you use with a dot.

A B C P S

2 Work out the total weight of each 3-fruit salad.

91

Cooking up problems

● **Use all four operations to solve word problems using one or more steps**

1 Work out the total weight of food in each bag.

a   b   c

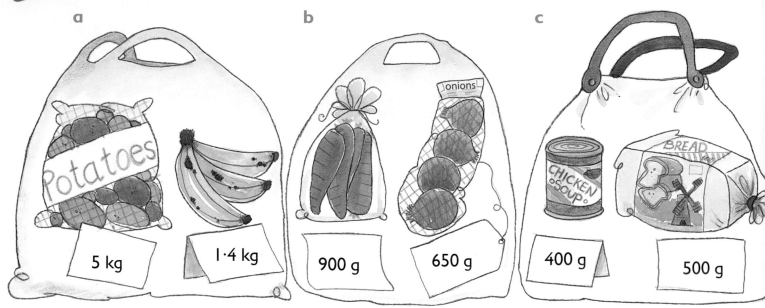

5 kg   1·4 kg   900 g   650 g   400 g   500 g

2 How much heavier is the bag of potatoes than the bag of carrots?

3 What is the approximate weight of one onion?

1 5 oranges weigh 1·25 kg. Simon eats one of them.
4 oranges weigh 0·95 kg.
What is the weight of the orange which he ate?

2 One egg weighs 70 g.
What is the weight of a box of six eggs?

3 Gran is making her special soup.
Here is her recipe.

$\frac{1}{4}$ bunch of celery

1 green pepper

$\frac{1}{2}$ bag of carrots

2 onions

1 tin of plum tomatoes

50 g mini pasta shells

Here is her shopping.

a Work out the weight of each vegetable which she uses.

b Find the total weight of vegetables which go into her soup.

4 Kenny has built this display of tins of dog food.

a What weight of dog food is in the display?

b He adds a fifth row of five cans. What does the food in the display now weigh?

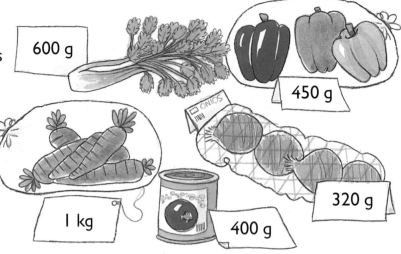

600 g

450 g

320 g

1 kg

400 g

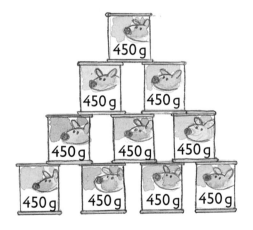

450 g

450 g   450 g

450 g   450 g   450 g

450 g   450 g   450 g   450 g

5 Carol's cat and its kitten weigh 2·6 kg. The cat weighs 1600 g more than its kitten. What is the weight of the kitten?

Strong plastic

1 Set up and carry out a test to see which shopping bag is the strongest. Make sure the test is fair.

2 Write a report of what you did.

You need:

● a spring balance or a measuring scale

● standard metric weights

● about 5 plastic shopping bags from different supermarkets and stores

Decimal sums and differences

● **Use knowledge of place value and addition and subtraction of two-digit numbers**

1 Use your knowledge of number facts for 10 to find the missing decimal.

I know 9 + 1 = 10
so 0·9 + 0·1 = 1.

a 0·4 ... ?

| 0 | 0·1 | 0·2 | 0·3 | 0·4 | 0·5 | 0·6 | 0·7 | 0·8 | 0·9 | |

b 0·8 ... ?

| 0 | 0·1 | 0·2 | 0·3 | 0·4 | 0·5 | 0·6 | 0·7 | 0·8 | 0·9 | |

c 0·5 ... ?

| 0 | 0·1 | 0·2 | 0·3 | 0·4 | 0·5 | 0·6 | 0·7 | 0·8 | 0·9 | |

d 0·1 ... ?

| 0 | 0·1 | 0·2 | 0·3 | 0·4 | 0·5 | 0·6 | 0·7 | 0·8 | 0·9 | |

e 0·3 ... ?

| 0 | 0·1 | 0·2 | 0·3 | 0·4 | 0·5 | 0·6 | 0·7 | 0·8 | 0·9 | |

f 0·7 ... ?

| 0 | 0·1 | 0·2 | 0·3 | 0·4 | 0·5 | 0·6 | 0·7 | 0·8 | 0·9 | |

g 0·2 ... ?

| 0 | 0·1 | 0·2 | 0·3 | 0·4 | 0·5 | 0·6 | 0·7 | 0·8 | 0·9 | |

2 Work with a partner. One of you says a decimal to one place and the other has to reply with the decimal that needs to be added to it to total 1. Take it in turns.

3 Now test yourself and see if you can write out all the pairs of decimals to one place that equal 1.

1 Use your knowledge of adding two-digit numbers to work out these calculations. Explain how you worked out the calculations.

a 0·54 + 0·37   b 0·28 + 0·45   c 0·39 + 0·52   d 0·49 + 0·84

e 0·39 + 0·76   f 0·84 + 0·83   g 0·62 + 0·29   h 0·87 + 0·37

i 0·45 + 0·68   j 0·57 + 0·77   k 0·36 + 0·95   l 0·08 + 0·87

2 Use your knowledge of subtracting two-digit numbers to work out these calculations. Explain how you worked out the calculations.

a 0·87 − 0·63   b 0·85 − 0·32   c 0·73 − 0·48   d 0·93 − 0·33

e 0·61 − 0·35   f 0·96 − 0·46   g 0·81 − 0·15   h 0·37 − 0·06

i 0·47 − 0·09   j 0·99 − 0·58   k 0·93 − 0·76   l 0·64 − 0·46

3 Choose five addition calculations from question **1** and five subtraction calculations from question **2**.
Write out the two-digit calculation that is similar.

4 Write a multiple of ten calculation that follows the same pattern.

What method would you use for these calculations?

a 3·26 + 2·87
b 6·92 + 8·14
c 12·63 + 16·49
d 13·55 − 7·23
e 8·82 − 1·66
f 17·06 − 11·83

How would you explain your method to someone who wasn't sure how to work them out?

Find the equivalent

Draw some circles like these. Then shade half of each one.

You need:
● paper and pencil

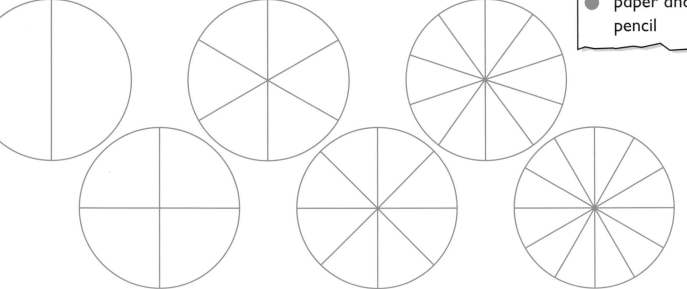

Underneath write the fraction that is equivalent to a half.

1 Look at these fractions and organise them into groups of equivalent fractions.

$\frac{1}{2}$ $\frac{3}{12}$ $\frac{2}{10}$ $\frac{5}{20}$ $\frac{2}{8}$ $\frac{4}{12}$ $\frac{4}{20}$ $\frac{1}{3}$

2 Explain how you worked out which fractions went together.

3 a Choose a fraction from the box and work out some equivalent fractions that go with it.

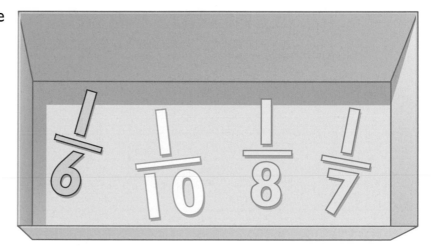

b Draw a diagram to show the equivalence between your fractions.

1 What do you need to think of when working out equivalent fractions?

2 What fractions are equivalent to $\frac{7}{49}$?

Using diagrams

● **Explain reasoning using diagrams**

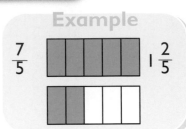

Example

$\frac{7}{5}$ $1\frac{2}{5}$

① Change these improper fractions to mixed numbers.
Use the diagrams to help you.

a $\frac{4}{3}$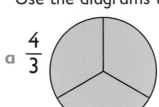

b $\frac{8}{6}$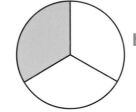

c $\frac{7}{4}$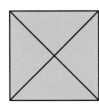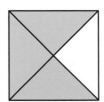

d $\frac{10}{8}$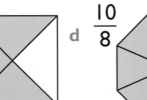

② Change these mixed numbers to improper fractions. Use the diagrams to help you.

a $1\frac{2}{6}$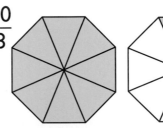

b $1\frac{3}{5}$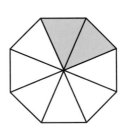

c $1\frac{9}{10}$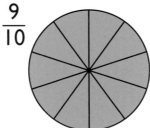

d $1\frac{3}{4}$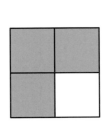

① Use the diagrams to help you change the improper fractions to mixed numbers and the mixed numbers to improper fractions.

a $\frac{7}{4}$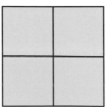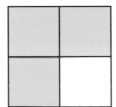

b $\frac{9}{5}$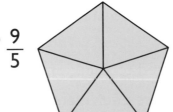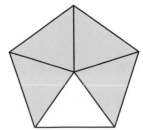

c $1\frac{2}{6}$

d $1\frac{3}{7}$

2 Draw a diagram to represent these improper fractions.

a $\frac{15}{8}$ b $\frac{4}{3}$ c $\frac{9}{8}$ d $\frac{13}{6}$ e $\frac{17}{4}$

f $\frac{11}{2}$ g $\frac{16}{5}$ h $\frac{20}{9}$ i $\frac{18}{10}$ j $\frac{121}{100}$

3 Change each of the improper fractions in question **2** into a mixed number.

4 Change these mixed numbers to improper fractions.

a $1\frac{3}{6}$ b $1\frac{4}{5}$ c $1\frac{2}{7}$ d $2\frac{4}{8}$ e $2\frac{1}{3}$

f $2\frac{6}{10}$ g $2\frac{8}{9}$ h $2\frac{7}{12}$ i $3\frac{3}{10}$ j $3\frac{18}{100}$

5 Why are diagrams helpful when converting mixed numbers and fractions?

I'm an improper fraction

$\frac{8}{6}$

$2\frac{2}{6}$

I'm a mixed number

Look back at your answers in the ⬤ activity.

a Write the mixed numbers from question **3** in order smallest to largest.

b Write the improper fractions from question **4** in order smallest to largest.

Find my partner

● **Relate fractions to their decimal equivalents**

 1 Match the decimals to their fraction partner.

0·5	$\frac{1}{10}$
0·1	$\frac{8}{10}$
0·8	$\frac{3}{10}$
0·2	$\frac{5}{10}$
0·6	$\frac{9}{10}$
0·9	$\frac{6}{10}$
0·4	$\frac{4}{10}$
0·7	$\frac{7}{10}$
0·3	$\frac{2}{10}$

2 Convert these decimals to their fraction equivalent.

4·5	6·7	8·1	5·3	4·7
12·8	14·6	9·2	15·4	17·9

 1 Match the decimals to their fraction partner.

$\frac{1}{4}$	0·3
$\frac{3}{4}$	0·74
$\frac{35}{100}$	0·5
$\frac{21}{100}$	0·75
$\frac{8}{10}$	0·25
$\frac{2}{10}$	0·35
$\frac{89}{100}$	0·8
$\frac{1}{2}$	0·89
$\frac{3}{10}$	0·21
$\frac{74}{100}$	0·2

2 Convert these fractions to their
decimal equivalent.

a $4\frac{6}{10}$ f $18\frac{3}{5}$

b $8\frac{63}{100}$ g $28\frac{26}{100}$

c $24\frac{3}{4}$ h $20\frac{9}{10}$

d $45\frac{1}{2}$ i $33\frac{1}{4}$

e $34\frac{2}{100}$ j $41\frac{89}{100}$

3 Convert these decimals to their
fraction equivalent.

a 5·64   f 26·75
b 3·78   g 14·2
c 9·4   h 20·42
d 24·5   i 3·09
e 11·06   j 26·7

Find as many fractions as you can equivalent to these decimal fractions.

0·5

0·25

0·2

0·75

Fractions, decimals and percentages

● **Express tenths and hundredths as percentages**

 Look at each grid and write down what fraction and what per cent is shaded.

a

b

c

> I can see 80 squares are shaded so that is 80%, $\frac{8}{10}$ or $\frac{4}{5}$.

d

e

f

g

h

i

j

Four in a row

A game for 2 players.

You need:
- about 15 counters all the same colour
- two 1-6 dice

1 Roll the dice and add up your score.

2 Look at the grid and see which fraction or its equivalent that you can cover.

3 Choose a square to cover.

4 The winner is the first person to get four counters in a row – horizontally, vertically or diagonally.

Dice	Fraction
2	$\frac{1}{2}$
3	$\frac{1}{10}$
4	$\frac{6}{10}$
5	$\frac{3}{4}$
6	$\frac{4}{10}$
7	$\frac{2}{10}$
8	$\frac{9}{10}$
9	$\frac{1}{4}$
10	$\frac{7}{10}$
11	$\frac{8}{10}$
12	$\frac{3}{10}$

$\frac{3}{4}$	50%	$\frac{8}{10}$	60%	$\frac{3}{10}$	$\frac{2}{10}$
0·5	$\frac{1}{10}$	80%	0·2	10%	70%
0·4	20%	0·1	$\frac{2}{10}$	0·25	0·2
$\frac{1}{4}$	0·7	$\frac{9}{10}$	0·6	$\frac{1}{2}$	30%
0·8	40%	0·3	$\frac{6}{10}$	25%	$\frac{7}{10}$
0·75	$\frac{4}{10}$	75%	0·9	90%	20%

I've rolled 6 so I can cover $\frac{4}{10}$ or 40% or 0·4.

Work out the equivalent fractions and decimals for these percentages.

a 15%	**b** 26%	**c** 33%	**d** 78%	**e** 82%
f 66%	**g** 58%	**h** 94%	**i** 120%	**j** 130%

Percentage problems

● **Find percentages of numbers and quantities**

1 Work out the percentages. Show all of your working.

a 50% of 100 cm

b 50% of £10

c 50% of 100 kg

d 50% of £1

e 50% of 10 m

f 25% of £1

g 25% of 100 m

h 25% of £100

i 25% of 100 kg

j 25% of £10

k 10% of 100 m

l 10% of £1

m 10% of 100 cm

n 10% of £100

o 10% of £10

2 Solve these percentage problems.

a 50% of the cake was eaten. What percentage was left?

b 80% of the children in Class 5 walk to school. What per cent do not walk to school?

c If I get 90% of questions right in a spelling test what per cent did I get wrong?

d In a maths test I scored 60 out of 100. What per cent did I get?

 Work out the percentages. Show all of your working.

1 a 25% of £80

b 25% of 44 m

c 25% of £24

d 25% of 60 kg

e 25% of £10

2 a 50% of 26 cm

b 50% of £48

c 50% of 500 kg

d 50% of £300

e 50% of 150 m

3 a 10% of 40 m
b 10% of £20
c 10% of 200 cm
d 10% of £150
e 10% of £90

4 a 75% of £16
b 75% of £40
c 75% of 200 m
d 75% of 80 kg
e 75% of 60 minutes

5 Solve these percentage problems.

a 70% of children at Woodlands School stay for lunch. What percentage do not stay?

b 23% of children in Class 5 say Maths is their favourite subject. How many do not prefer maths?

c A survey of favourite colours was done. 25% of people asked said red was their favourite colour and 14% said blue was their favourite. What percentage did not like red or blue best?

d In a maths test I scored 40 marks out of 80 and my friend scored 45% of 80. Who did the best – me or my friend?

Write five word problems using these percentages for a friend to work out.
a 25% of £148
b 10% of 350
c 60% of 30 km
d 75% of 60 minutes
e 40% of 120 g

In proportion

● **Solve problems involving proportions of quantities**

 ① For every 1p Ian saves, his brother Gavin saves 5p.
Copy and complete the table.

Ian	Gavin
1p	5p

② For every 1 chocolate bar Chris eats, Karen eats 3.
Copy and complete the table.

Chris	Karen
1	3

③ When we go swimming, for every one length I swim,
my friend swims 4. Copy and complete the table.

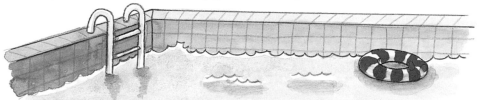

Me	My friend
1	4

① Cereal bars come in packs of 8. Out of every packet,
I eat 7 cereal bars and my mum eats one. Copy and
complete the table.

a How many cereal bars have I eaten
   if my mum has eaten 5?
b How many cereal bars has my
   mum eaten if I have eaten 49?
c What proportion of the cereal bars do I eat?

Me	Mum
7	1
14	

2 For every 5 minutes I spend tidying my room, I can watch 10 minutes of television. Copy and complete the table.

Tidying room	TV
5	10
10	

a Tonight I can watch 60 minutes of television. How much time did I spend tidying my room?

b If I spend 40 minutes tidying my room, for how long will I be able to watch television?

c What proportion of time do I spend watching TV?

3 Every time I buy 2 goldfish for my pond, I buy 4 new plants. Copy and complete the table showing the proportion of fish to plants in my pond.

Fish	Plants
2	4

a When I have 48 plants how many fish will there be?

b If I get 20 fish how many plants will I need?

54 tiles can fit on my kitchen floor. I want to put 3 blue tiles for every 6 white tiles.
How many of each colour tile will I need to buy?
Use a 6 × 9 piece of squared paper to plan my kitchen floor.

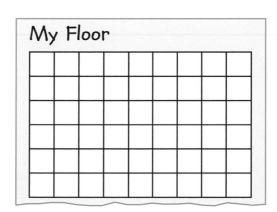

My Floor

You need:
- 1 cm squared paper
- ruler
- blue pencil

Use the proportion

● **Solve problems involving proportions of quantities**

Work out the problems. You may want to copy and complete the table to help you.

1 Rachel is mixing pink paint. For every spoonful of red paint she puts in 4 spoonfuls of white.
If she puts in 7 spoonfuls of red how many white will she put in?

Red	White
1	4
2	
3	
4	
5	
6	
7	

2 Tim is feeding his cat and her kitten sweets. For every 1 sweet he gives the kitten, he gives the cat 3. He has 24 sweets to share. How many will they each have?

Cat	Kitten
3	1

3 Dad has made 6 cakes. On every cake he puts 1 cherry and 2 chocolate chips. How many of each will he need?

Cherries	Choc chips
1	2

Work out the problems using the proportions given. Show all your working.

1 There are 30 children going on the school outing. For every 2 boys going there are 4 girls. How many boys and how many girls are going?

2 In every bag of apples you buy, there are 2 red apples and 5 green. I buy 4 bags. How many of each colour apple will I have?

3 In the staffroom, for every one cup of tea drunk, seven cups of coffee are drunk. Today 5 cups of tea have been drunk. How many cups of coffee have been drunk?

4 A box of chocolates has 3 toffee-filled chocolates for every 5 nut-filled ones. I buy a box of 24 chocolates. How many of each chocolate will I have?

5 At Park Vale school, for every 6 children, 4 wear uniform and 2 do not. In one class of 30 how many children will be wearing uniform and how many will not?

I am making a tablecloth by sewing squares together. For every 3 orange squares I have 2 red. Altogether I have 50 squares.
a Design my tablecloth.
b What fraction of the tablecloth is red?
c What fraction of the tablecloth is orange?
d What percentage of the tablecloth is red?
e What percentage of the tablecloth is orange?

You need:
● 1 cm squared paper
● ruler
● red and orange pencils

Divide and share

● **Find fractions using division of numbers and quantities**

Mr. Splinter, the carpenter, has a piece of wood 48 m long. He wants to saw it up into smaller pieces. He wants the pieces to be whole metres.

Copy this table into your book to help you decide how many ways he could saw it up. Before you start your working out for each problem, make some predictions.

My predictions

Numbers I try	Calculation	Length of each piece	Fraction
2	48 ÷ 2 = 24	24 m	$\frac{1}{2}$

Solve the problems using a calculator. Before you start your working out for each problem, make some predictions. You need to draw a table in your book for each problem that will show your predictions, your working and your answers.

1 Mrs. Flour, the baker, has baked a chocolate roll that is 192 cm long. She is deciding how to cut it up. She can only measure whole centimetres and wants all the pieces to be exactly the same.

a What choices does she have?

b What fractions will each choice divide the roll into?

c If you were Mrs. Flour which option would you choose and why?

2 Mr. Bark, the gardener, has had 378 kg of soil delivered. He needs to put it into sacks to sell it. His scales can only weigh whole kilograms. Each sack must hold exactly the same amount.

He wants to have at least 10 sacks of soil and not more than 30.

a What choices does he have?

b What fraction of the whole amount will each bag hold?

c How do you know you have found all the possible options?

Mrs. Sparkle, the jeweller, had a delivery of diamonds. She put a quarter of them in the safe. She used a tenth of them to make rings. She sold three fifths of them to another jeweller for a profit. She was left with a twentieth of the diamonds which she used to make herself a necklace. Her necklace contained four diamonds.

a How many diamonds did she have delivered?

b How many were in the safe?

c How many were used for rings?

d How many did she sell?

You need:
● calculator

Calculating costs

Use a calculator to solve problems involving decimals

Use your calculator to work out these calculations.

a £1·32 + £2·51

b £9·63 + £4·11

c £3·85 + £5·19

d £1·97 + £4·80

e £6·59 + £2·75

f £19·99 – £8·52

g £3·01 – £1·03

h £24·62 – £16·50

i 3 × £1·24

j 5 × £3·99

k 2 × £51·73

l 7 × £2·01

m £6·25 ÷ 5

n £12·34 ÷ 2

o £5·44 ÷ 4

p £42·67 ÷ 17

Football £8·40

Boomerang £6·35

Rocket £15·21

Aeroplane £14·99

Frisbee £5·60

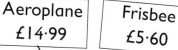

1 Calculate the cost of:

a

b

c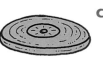

2 Calculate the difference in price between:

a

b

c

3 Calculate the total cost of:

a

b

c

4 Find the change from a £20 note if you buy:

a

b

c

5 Find the total cost for each shopping bill.

a
apples	£2·34
bread	£1·63
eggs	£1·99
meat	£3·06
Total	_____

b
tissues	£1·30
clingfilm	£2·05
scourers	£1·76
washing powder	£3·99
Total	_____

c
drinks	£9·32
DVD	£5·00
chicken	£6·40
crisps	£1·28
nuts	£3·00
Total	_____

6 The total cost of these objects is shown. Calculate the cost of one object.

 £2·76

 £9·90

 £7

You need:
● calculator

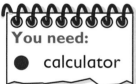 £4·16

 £2·60

 £1·28

 £1·83

 £11·41

 £8·99

1 You have a £5 note to spend.
Buy some of these items and work out the change.

2 Buy more items with another £5 note. Spend as much as you can. Work out the change.

3 Start with a £10 note. Repeat question **2**.

4 Start with a £20 note. Repeat question **2**.

 £1·75

Doubling multiplication facts

● **Use doubling to multiply by 12, 14, 16 and 18**

Copy and complete the multiplication table.

Example

6 × 5

×	5	8	2	6	4	3	1	9	7	10
6	3 0									
8										
7										
9										

1 Multiply each of these numbers by 16.

Use the 8 times table to help you.

Example

4 × 16
= (4 × 8) + (4 × 8)
= 32 + 32
= 64

2 Multiply each of these numbers by 12.

Use the 6 times table to help you.

Example

9 × 12
= (9 × 6) + (9 × 6)
= 54 + 54
= 108

3 Multiply each of these numbers by 14.

Use the 7 times table to help you.

Example

7×14
$= (7 \times 7) + (7 \times 7)$
$= 49 + 49$
$= 98$

4 Multiply each of these numbers by 18.

Use the 9 times table to help you.

Example

6×18
$= (6 \times 9) + (6 \times 9)$
$= 54 + 54$
$= 108$

Copy and complete the multiplication table.

Example

23×16
$= (23 \times 8) + (23 \times 8)$
$= 184 + 184$
$= 368$

×	16	18	12	14
23	3 6 8			
46				
58				
72				
37				

Doubling and halving whole numbers and decimals

● **Double and halve whole numbers and decimals**

- Take turns to roll the dice twice and make two two-digit numbers, e.g. 4 and 2 makes 42 and 24.
- Double one of the numbers and halve the other, e.g. $42 \times 2 = 84$ and $24 \div 2 = 12$.
- Now add both numbers together, e.g. $84 + 12 = 96$.
- That is your score for that round.
- The winner of each round is the player with the greater total.
- Play 10 rounds.

You need:
- 2 × 0-9 dice
- pencil and paper

- Take turns to roll the dice twice and make two decimal numbers, each with one decimal place, e.g. 8 and 5 makes 8·5 and 5·8.
- Double one of the decimals and halve the other, e.g. $8·5 \times 2 = 17$ and $5·8 \div 2 = 2·9$.
- Now add both decimals together, e.g. $17 + 2·9 = 19·9$.
- That is your score for that round.
- The winner of each round is the player with the greater total.
- Play 10 rounds.

You need:
- 2 × 0-9 dice
- pencil and paper

- Take turns to roll the dice twice and make two decimal numbers, each with no units and two decimal places, e.g. 7 and 3 makes 0·73 and 0·37.
- Double one of the decimals and halve the other, e.g. $0·73 \times 2 = 1·46$ and $0·37 \div 2 = 0·185$.
- Now add both decimals together, e.g. $1·46 + 0·185 = 1·645$.
- That is your score for that round.
- The winner of each round is the player with the greater total.
- Play 10 rounds.

You need:

- 2 × 0–9 dice
- pencil and paper

Exchange rates

Make simple conversions of pounds to foreign currency

 1 What currency is used in:

a Spain
b Thailand
c France
d Ireland
e Australia?

3 Which country uses the currency:

a rupee
b yen
c rand
d shekel
e krone?

What is the exchange rate for the:

a Danish krone
b Turkish lirasi
c Malaysia ringgit
d US dollar
e New Zealand dollar?

2 Which countries use:

a dollars
b €?

Tourist rates			
Australia ($)	2·57	Malaysia (ringgit)	5·72
Austria (€)	1·56	Mexico (nuevo peso)	13·42
Belgium (€)	1·56	New Zealand ($)	3·09
Canada ($)	2·25	Norway (krone)	13·61
Denmark (krone)	12·49	Portugal (€)	1·56
Finland (€)	9·98	Saudi Arabia (riyal)	5·72
France (€)	1·56	Singapore ($)	2·55
Germany (€)	1·56	South Africa (rand)	10·31
Hong Kong ($)	11·80	Spain (€)	1·56
Ireland (€)	1·56	Sweden (krona)	13·67
India (rupee)	61·55	Thailand (baht)	54·92
Israel (shekel)	5·84	Turkey (lirasi)	930 029
Italy (€)	1·56	USA ($)	1·52
Japan (yen)	165·21		

1 Answer these questions about exchange rates.

a Why are exchange rates also referred to as 'tourist rates'?
b What information does the tourist rate give us?
c Why does the tourist rate appear in the newspaper on a daily basis?
d What are the main reasons people need to know how much the pound is worth in other currencies?
e What does an exchange rate of 10·42 mean?

2 The Phillips family are deciding where to go on holiday. Copy and complete the table to find out how much of each currency they would receive if they exchanged £5, £10 or £20. Use the tourist rates shown in the ▢ activity.

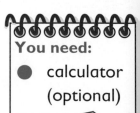

You need:
● calculator (optional)

Country	Currency	Exchange Rate	£5 =	£10 =	£20 =
Australia					
Denmark					
India					
Mexico					
South Africa					
Thailand					
Canada					
Hong Kong					
Japan					
Singapore					
USA					
New Zealand					

The Phillips family bought some items on their round-the-world holiday. Use the exchange rates in the activity to work out the cost of each item in British pounds. Give your answer in pounds and pence.

You need:
● calculator

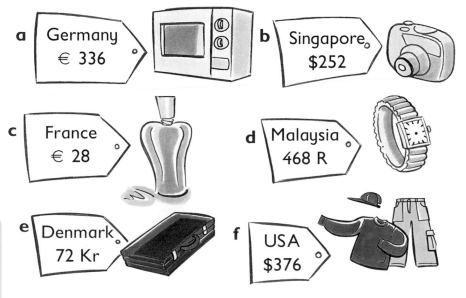

a Germany € 336

b Singapore $252

c France € 28

d Malaysia 468 R

e Denmark 72 Kr

f USA $376

Using a calculator

- Develop calculator skills and use a calculator effectively
- Order a set of positive and negative integers

1 Copy and complete the number lines.

You need:
- calculator

a

−4 ☐ −2 ☐ 0 1 ☐ ☐ ☐ ☐

b

☐ −5 ☐ −3 ☐ −1 0 ☐ 2 3 ☐

c

☐ −7 ☐ −5 ☐ ☐ −2 −1 0 1 ☐

d

☐ ☐ ☐ ☐ 0 ☐ 2 ☐ ☐ 5

2 Use the constant function on your calculator to count. Press the equals key ten times. Write down all the numbers the calculator displays.

a Starting at **0** count on in **2**s.
c Starting at **0** count on in **3**s.
b Starting at **0** count on in **1**s.
d Starting at **40** count back in **4**s.

 1 Write these numbers in descending order.

a −4, −3, −8, −1, 0, −9
b 6, −7, 1, −2, 3, −6
c 0, 10, −1, 4, 7, −7
d 7, −4, 6, −8, 5, 1
e −3, 2, 0, −11, −8, 5
f −2, −8, −6, 5, 8, 12

You need:
- calculator

2 Use the constant function on your calculator to count. Press the equals key ten times. Write down all the numbers the calculator displays.

a Starting at **0** count on in **8**s.

b Starting at **3** count on in **2**s.

c Starting at **5 0** count back in **5**s.

d Starting at **2** count back in **1**s.

e Starting at **0** count back in **2**s.

f Starting at **1 0 0** count back in **3**s.

g Starting at **7 1** count back in **2**s.

h Starting at **7** count on in **5**s.

i Starting at **8 1** count back in **9**s.

j Starting at **1** count on in **1 1**s.

▶ Up and down

You can do this on your own or with a partner.

1 Write the numbers 1 to 9 on a sheet of paper.

2 Choose one of the numbers and decide whether to add or subtract it from one of the other numbers.

3 Cross the numbers out as you use them.

4 Keep going until you have used all the numbers.

5 The aim is to reach −9 exactly.

You need:

● pencil and paper

● calculator

Number puzzles

 Find different combinations of two numbers on each shape to make the totals shown.

a

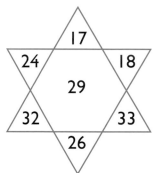

17
24   18
29
32   33
26

Total = 50

b

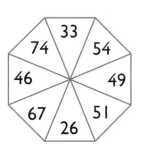

33
74   54
46   49
67   51
26

Total = 100

c

11
22   27
39
46   28
4

Total = 50

d

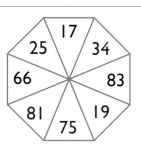

17
25   34
66   83
81   19
75

Total = 100

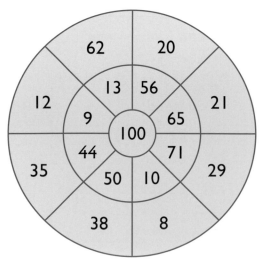

62   20
13 56
12
9   65
21
100
44   71
35
50 10   29
38   8

1 Total = 100

● Find as many ways of making 100 as possible.

● Choose two numbers from the board that add up to 100.

● Find as many more pairs as you can.

● Choose any three numbers from the board that add up to 100.

● Find as many more sets of three numbers as you can.

● Choose any four numbers from the board that add up to 100.

● Find as many more sets of four numbers as you can.

122

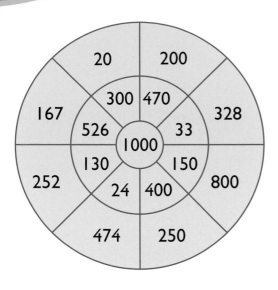

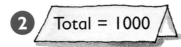

Total = 1000

● Find as many ways of making 1000 as possible.

● Choose any two numbers from the board that add up to 1000.

● Find as many more pairs as you can.

● Choose any three numbers from the board that add up to 1000.

● Find as many more sets of three numbers as you can.

● Choose any four numbers from the board that add up to 1000.

● Find as many more sets of four numbers as you can.

❶ Double the numbers on the outer ring each time you use them.

❷ Make your own number wheel.

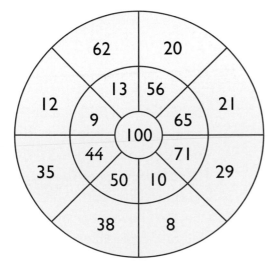

Choose any numbers on the board to find different ways of making 100.

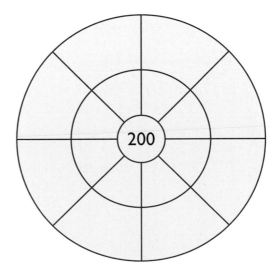

Choose 16 numbers that when added together in combinations of 2, 3 or 4 give the total 200.

Maths Facts

Problem solving

The seven steps to problem solving

1 Read the problem carefully. **2** What do you have to find?

3 What facts are given? **4** Which of the facts do you need?

5 Make a plan. **6** Carry out your plan to obtain your answer. **7** Check your answer.

Number

Positive and negative numbers

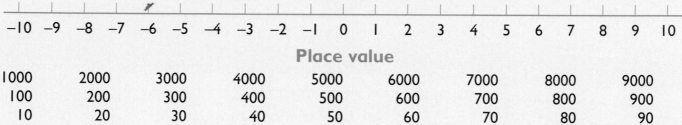

$$-10 \quad -9 \quad -8 \quad -7 \quad -6 \quad -5 \quad -4 \quad -3 \quad -2 \quad -1 \quad 0 \quad 1 \quad 2 \quad 3 \quad 4 \quad 5 \quad 6 \quad 7 \quad 8 \quad 9 \quad 10$$

Place value

1000	2000	3000	4000	5000	6000	7000	8000	9000
100	200	300	400	500	600	700	800	900
10	20	30	40	50	60	70	80	90
1	2	3	4	5	6	7	8	9
0·1	0·2	0·3	0·4	0·5	0·6	0·7	0·8	0·9
0·01	0·02	0·03	0·04	0·05	0·06	0·07	0·08	0·09
0·001	0·002	0·003	0·004	0·005	0·006	0·007	0·008	0·009

Fractions, decimals and percentages

$\frac{1}{100} = 0·01 = 1\%$ $\qquad$ $\frac{2}{100} = \frac{1}{50} = 0·02 = 2\%$ $\qquad$ $\frac{5}{100} = \frac{1}{20} = 0·05 = 5\%$

$\frac{10}{100} = \frac{1}{10} = 0·1 = 10\%$ $\qquad$ $\frac{1}{8} = 0·125 = 12·5\%$ $\qquad$ $\frac{20}{100} = \frac{1}{5} = 0·2 = 20\%$

$\frac{25}{100} = \frac{1}{4} = 0·25 = 25\%$ $\qquad$ $\frac{1}{3} = 0·333 = 33\frac{1}{3}\%$ $\qquad$ $\frac{50}{100} = \frac{1}{2} = 0·5 = 50\%$

$\frac{2}{3} = 0·667 = 66\frac{2}{3}\%$ $\qquad$ $\frac{75}{100} = \frac{3}{4} = 0·75 = 75\%$ $\qquad$ $\frac{100}{100} = 1 = 100\%$

Number facts

Multiplication and division facts

	×1	×2	×3	×4	×5	×6	×7	×8	×9	×10
×1	1	2	3	4	5	6	7	8	9	10
×2	2	4	6	8	10	12	14	16	18	20
×3	3	6	9	12	15	18	21	24	27	30
×4	4	8	12	16	20	24	28	32	36	40
×5	5	10	15	20	25	30	35	40	45	50
×6	6	12	18	24	30	36	42	48	54	60
×7	7	14	21	28	35	42	49	56	63	70
×8	8	16	24	32	40	48	56	64	72	80
×9	9	18	27	36	45	54	63	72	81	90
×10	10	20	30	40	50	60	70	80	90	100

Tests of divisibility

2 The last digit is 0, 2, 4, 6 or 8.

3 The sum of the digits is divisible by 3.

4 The last two digits are divisible by 4.

5 The last digit is 5 or 0.

6 It is divisible by both 2 and 3.

7 Check a known near multiple of 7.

8 Half of it is divisible by 4 *or*
The last 3 digits are divisible by 8.

9 The sum of the digits is divisible by 9.

10 The last digit is 0.

Calculations

Addition

Whole numbers
Example: 6845 + 5758

```
   6845                    6845
 + 5758                  + 5758
  11 000                  12 603
   1 500                    1 1 1
     90
     13
  12 603
     1
```

Decimals
Example: 26.48 + 5.375

```
  26.48                   26.48
 + 5.375                 + 5.375
  20.000                  31.855
  11.000                    1  1
   0.700
   0.150
   0.005
  31.855
```

Subtraction

Whole numbers
Example: 7845 − 2367

```
  7845      or           700   130   15        7 13 15
 − 2367                  700   140    5          7̶8̶4̶5̶
    33 → 2400     7000 + 800 + 40 + 5          − 2367
  5445 → 7845   − 2000 + 300 + 60 + 7            5478
  5478           5000 + 400 + 70 + 8
```

Decimals
Example: 639.35 − 214.46

```
  639.35      or               8 12 15
 − 214.46                    6̶3̶9̶.3̶5̶
   00.54 → 215             − 214.46
  424.35 → 639.35            424.89
  424.89
```

Multiplication

Whole numbers
Example: 5697 × 8

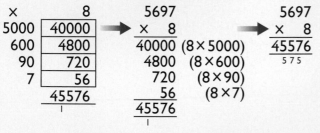

```
  ×        8          5697            5697
5000  | 40000 |       ×  8            ×  8
 600  |  4800 |       40000 (8×5000)  45576
  90  |   720 |        4800 (8×600)    5 7 5
   7  |    56 |         720 (8×90)
        45576            56 (8×7)
          1            45576
                          1
```

Decimals
Example: 865.56 × 7

```
  ×        7          865.56          865.56
 800  | 5600 |        ×    7          ×    7
  60  |  420 |        5600  (7×800)   6058.92
   5  |   35 |         420  (7× 60)    4 3 3 4
0.50  |  3.5 |          35  (7×  5)
0.06  | 0.42 |         3.5  (7×  0.50)
       6058.92         0.42 (7×  0.06)
          1          6058.92
                        1
```

Whole numbers
Example: 364 × 87

```
  ×  |  80   |  7              364                    364
300  | 24000 | 2100   26100   ×  87                  ×  87
 60  |  4800 |  420    5220    24000  (300×80)        29120   364 × 80
  4  |   320 |   28     348     4800  (60×80)          2548   364 ×  7
                       31668     320  (4×80)          31668
                         1      2100  (300× 7)            1
                                 420  (60× 7)
                                  28  (4× 7)
                                31668
                                 1 1
```

Calculations

Division

Whole numbers

Example: 337 ÷ 8

```
8) 337
 -  80    (8 × 10)
   257
 -  80    (8 × 10)
   177
 -  80    (8 × 10)
    97
 -  80    (8 × 10)
    17
 -  16    (8 × 2)
     1     42
```

Answer   42 R 1

```
8) 337
 - 320    (8 × 40)
    17
 -  16    (8 × 2)
     1     42
```

Answer   42 R 1

```
      42   R 1
8) 337
   32
   17
   16
    1
```

```
      42   R 1
8) 33⁷7
```

Decimals

Example: 78.3 ÷ 9

```
9) 78.3
 - 72.0    (9 × 8)
    6.3
 -  6.3    (9 × 0.7)
      0     8.7)
```

Answer   8.7

Example: 48.6 ÷ 3

```
3) 48.6
 - 30.0    (3 × 10)
   18.6
 - 18.0    (3 × 6)
    0.6
 -  0.6    (3 × 0.2)
      0    16.2
```

Answer   16.2

Order of operations

Brackets ➡ Division ➡ Multiplication ➡ Addition ➡ Subtraction

Shape and space

2–D shapes

 circle

 semi-circle

 right-angled triangle

 equilateral triangle

 isosceles triangle

 scalene triangle

 square

 rectangle

 rhombus

 kite

 parallelogram

 trapezium

 pentagon

 hexagon

 heptagon

octagon

Shape and space

3–D solids

 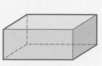

cube   cuboid   cone   cylinder   sphere   hemi-sphere

triangular prism   triangular-based pyramid (tetrahedron)   square-based pyramid   octahedron   dodecahedron

Co-ordinates

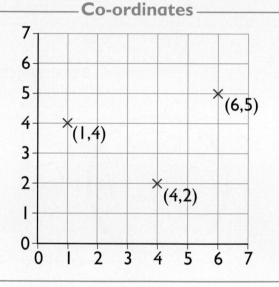

Reflection

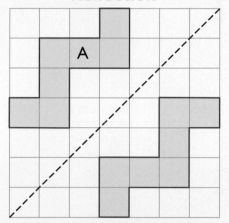

Shape A has been reflected along the diagonal line of symmetry

Rotation

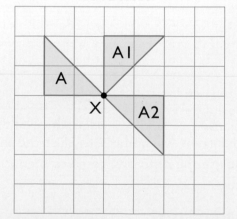

Shape A has been rotated through 90° (Shape A1) and 180° (Shape A2) around Point X

Translation

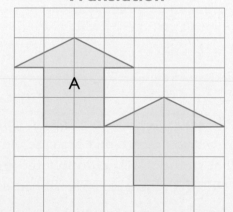

Shape A has been translated 3 squares to the right and 2 squares down.

Shape and space

Angles

Acute angle < 90°
Obtuse angle > 90° and < 180°
Reflex angle > 180° and < 360°
4 right angles (complete turn) = 360°

Right angle = 90°
Straight angle = 180°

Lines

Parallel lines

Perpendicular lines

Measures

Length

1 km	=	1000 m	=	100 000 cm		
0·1 km	=	100 m	=	10 000 cm	=	100 000 mm
0·01 km	=	10 m	=	1000 cm	=	10 000 mm
1 m	=	100 cm	=	1000 mm		
0·1 m	=	10 cm	=	100 mm		
0·01 m	=	1 cm	=	10 mm		
1 cm	=	10 mm		0·1 cm	=	1 mm

Mass

1 t	=	1000 kg	1 kg	=	1000 g
0.1 kg	=	100 g	0.01 kg	=	10 g

Capacity

1 litre	=	1000 ml	0.1 l	=	100 ml
0.01 l	=	10 ml	1 cl	=	10 ml

Metric units and imperial units

Length

8 km ≈ 5 miles (1 mile ≈ 1.6 km)

Mass

1 kg ≈ 2.2 lb
30 g ≈ 1 oz

Capacity

1 litre ≈ $1\frac{3}{4}$ pints
4.5 litres ≈ 8 pints (1 gallon)

Time

1 millennium	=	1000 years
1 century	=	100 years
1 decade	=	10 years
1 year	=	12 months
	=	365 days
	=	366 days (leap year)
1 week (wk)	=	7 days
1 day	=	24 hours
1 minute (min)	=	60 seconds

24 hour time

Perimeter and Area

P = perimeter   A = area   l = length   b = breadth

Perimeter of a rectangle:
P = 2l + 2b or P = 2 x (l + b)

Perimeter of a square:
P = 4 x l

Area of a rectangle:
A = l x b

Handling data

Planning an investigation

❶ Describe your investigation. ❷ Do you have a prediction? ❸ Describe the data you need to collect.
❹ How will you record and organise the data? ❺ What diagrams will you use to illustrate the data?
❻ What statistics will you calculate? ❼ How will you analyse the data and come to a conclusion?
❽ When you have finished, describe how your investigation could be improved.

Mode
The value that occurs most often.

Range
Difference between the largest value and the smallest value.

Median
Middle value when all the values have been ordered smallest to largest.

Mean
Total of all the values divided by the number of values.